TRIPLE
CROWNED

JOSE CARLOS FAJARDO/STAFF

The San Francisco Giants' Incredible 2014 Championship Season

This book is book is available in quantity at special discounts for your group or organization. For further information, contact:

Triumph Books LLC
814 North Franklin Street
Chicago, Illinois 60610
Phone: (312) 337-0747
www.triumphbooks.com

Printed in U.S.A.
ISBN: 978-1-62937-055-2

Bay Area News Group
Sharon Ryan, Publisher and President, Bay Area News Group
David J. Butler, Editor and Vice President for News, MediaNewsGroup
Bert Robinson, Managing Editor, Bay Area News Group
Bud Geracie, Executive Sports Editor, Bay Area News Group

Content packaged by Mojo Media, Inc.
Joe Funk: Editor
Jason Hinman: Creative Director

Front cover photo by Jose Carlos Fajardo/Staff. Back cover photo by Nhat V. Meyer/Staff.

NHAT V. MEYER/STAFF

CONTENTS

INTRODUCTION

By Alex Pavlovic

Hunter Pence stood at a computer in the center of the visitors' clubhouse at Petco Park and started to click through YouTube videos. The Giants were in the midst of a slump that so often made this season seem like a long, hard road to an October tee time.

There were nights when scoring one run at AT&T Park was cause for celebration and others when the vaunted pitching staff looked in need of a rebuild. There was the day Matt Cain was officially lost to elbow surgery and the day that Angel Pagan had season-ending back surgery. Almost every day was spent without Marco Scutaro, the anticipated starter at second base.

But on this night in San Diego, Pence found the clip he was looking for and hit play on an anthem that became the soundtrack of the 2014 World Cup.

"I believe that we will win! I believe that we will win! I believe that we will win!"

It rumbled through the speakers as Pence walked slowly back to his locker and sat down, faith restored.

Above all, the 2014 Giants relied on that faith. Oh, there was talent, plenty of it. They had an ace, Madison Bumgarner, who turned into one of the biggest World Series stars in history, and a starting staff filled with veterans who never shied away from the moment. The bullpen had a core four — Santiago Casilla, Jeremy Affeldt, Sergio Romo and Javier Lopez — that was unhittable

and a long man — Yusmeiro Petit — who practically shut out October. The Giants had a lineup buoyed by Pence's hustle, Buster Posey's persistence, Joe Panik's poise, Pablo Sandoval's timing and the power of Michael Morse and Brandon Belt. The defense was solid at all times and stepped up to spectacular when Brandon Crawford or Gregor Blanco got involved.

But through the ups and downs of a marathon season, it was faith that provided the foundation. Bruce Bochy told his players they had "Champions Blood," and they believed it. They believed that blood coursed through their veins from the first workout in Arizona till the final pitch in Kansas City.

The faith in the winning system was why Tim Hudson and Morse chose San Francisco, and both were instrumental as the Giants stormed out a to 10-game lead in the National League West and the best record in baseball through two months. They were 44-24 as late as June 12. One night during that stretch, Crawford leaned against his locker in the victors' clubhouse at Dodger Stadium and smiled.

"This kind of reminds me of the 2012 team," he said.

From that high point, the Giants morphed into the disappointing 2013 team. They lost 22 of 30 home games in the middle of the summer, relegating themselves to the race for the dreaded one-or-done wild-card game.

PABLO SANDOVAL EXULTS AFTER CATCHING THE FINAL OUT OF GAME 7 TO CLINCH THE 2014 WORLD SERIES TITLE FOR THE GIANTS. (D. ROSS CAMERON/STAFF)

It was ugly baseball at times, and the Giants admitted it. But even that stretch couldn't shake the faith that better times were ahead. Morse stood over reporters at his locker one day and laughed off a question about frustration.

"The only people frustrated are you guys," he said. "We've got 25 guys in here coming in every day to play to win. There's no stopping that. That's what we do."

They never did it consistently down the stretch, but the Giants won enough in August and September to sneak into the wild-card game. It wasn't hard to find faith at that point. Bumgarner had won a career-high 18 games and made his second All-Star team, and those poor Pittsburgh Pirates stood no chance. Bumgarner threw a shutout and Crawford grand-slammed the Giants into a matchup with the Washington Nationals, widely believed to be the best team in the National League.

No Giants player spoke more openly about faith than Jake Peavy, the trade-deadline acquisition who went 1-9 in Boston and then 6-4 with a 2.17 ERA down the stretch as Cain's replacement. "Boch and these guys believed that I could be that guy, and when you are shown that faith in you, you want to exhaust every option," Peavy said. "That really can fuel a fire."

Peavy ignited the Giants in their opener of the NLDS in Washington. One out away from losing Game 2, the Giants got a hard-worked walk from Panik, a rookie unimpressed by the moment, and then a game-tying hit from Sandoval. Petit, a late-season replacement in the rotation, threw six brilliant innings until Belt's 18th inning homer ended the longest postseason game in MLB history.

The Giants took that series in four games and won the next one in five. Where others saw luck pushing San Francisco past St. Louis, the clubhouse saw execution and a will to win. A Cardinals misplay led to one Giants victory and two Cardinals misplays helped win another game.

"Rocks and slingshots," third base coach Tim Flannery said. "We can score runs without hits. We've proven that."

The Giants would get hits in the clincher against St. Louis, big ones. Morse had missed six weeks with an oblique strain, but his pinch-hit home run in the eighth inning gave the Giants new life. There was no stronger example of faith than Travis Ishikawa, the former Giant who nearly retired but instead took one last minor-league shot with the organization that drafted him. In the ninth inning, Ishikawa blasted a fastball into the dark night and the Giants walked off into the World Series.

"It's so gratifying," an emotional Ishikawa said. "I'm so happy I was able to do it for this city and this team."

The Giants were hardly finished. Bumgarner rolled the Kansas City Royals in Game 1 of the World Series, then restored the Giants' series lead with a Game 5 shutout. That was just the warm-up. In Game 7, two nights after throwing 117 pitches, Bumgarner came out of the bullpen with five more scoreless innings to nail down a 3-2 victory and clinch the third championship in five years.

A dynasty was born, one the rest of baseball never saw coming. Only the Giants did.

"Honestly," Belt said with a shrug. "We just know how to win."

And they always believed that they would. ∎

HUNTER PENCE SCORES ON BRANDON CRAWFORD'S SECOND-INNING SACRIFICE FLY TO GIVE THE GIANTS AN EARLY 2-0 LEAD IN GAME 7. (JOSIE LEPE/STAFF)

WORLD SERIES: GAME 1

OCTOBER 21, 2014 | GIANTS 7, ROYALS 1

A ROYAL FLUSHING

S.F. HANDS ROYALS THEIR FIRST LOSS OF THE 2014 POSTSEASON WITH A 7-RUN EXPLOSION

BY ALEX PAVLOVIC

KANSAS CITY, MO.—The downfall of the ace this postseason has been swift and nearly universal.

Clayton Kershaw crouching on the mound in St. Louis. Stephen Strasburg looking on from the visiting dugout at AT&T Park as the Giants sent him home. Adam Wainwright doing the same a round later. And Kansas City Royals ace James "Big Game" Shields looking for a new nickname.

And yet here was Madison Bumgarner on Tuesday night, the last ace standing, adding to his legend. The 25-year-old threw seven more stellar innings to lead the Giants to a 7-1 win over the Royals in Game 1 of the World Series.

He is 3-0 with a 0.41 ERA in three World Series starts and 3-1 with a 1.40 ERA this October while starting five of the Giants' 11 games and throwing at least seven innings each time. This postseason has humbled one big name after the next, but Bumgarner is better than he has ever been.

"There is no bigger stage," right fielder Hunter Pence said. "But he's just Madison Bumgarner."

Right now, he's not just Madison Bumgarner. He's the best big-game pitcher in a sport that wears you down over 162 games and then forms your legacy with snapshots taken as the weather cools. The Giants didn't particularly need Bumgarner to be brilliant in Game 1, not with the lineup jumping on Shields.

But with the sporting world watching, Bumgarner grabbed hold of another opportunity to send a message. The Royals had not lost this postseason, but Bumgarner limited them to three hits and a lone run that came long after the game was out of hand. He mixed 94 mph fastballs with 67 mph curveballs and made such quick work of the Royals that it wasn't worth comparing him to Shields or his other contemporaries. Bumgarner's main competition this month has been the record book.

He threw a record 32⅔ consecutive scoreless postseason innings on the road before Salvador Perez whacked a fastball into the home bullpen in the seventh. That shot also snapped Bumgarner's run of 21 straight scoreless World Series innings to begin his career, the second-longest streak in history. When the only man ahead of you on a list is Hall of Famer Christy Mathewson (28 innings), you're doing just fine.

"I'm not here trying to set records and keep streaks going and whatever, but you do know about it," he said. "A World Series game is not something you exactly forget about."

This was the first one here in 29 years, and the city

MADISON BUMGARNER DELIVERS A PITCH IN THE SIXTH INNING OF GAME 1. THE LEFTHANDER EARNED THE WIN, HIS SIXTH CAREER POSTSEASON VICTORY, SETTING A FRANCHISE RECORD. (NHAT V. MEYER/STAFF)

bathed in blue in preparation for the matchup. The Giants took the air out of Kauffman Stadium right away, and they did it using a playbook that was supposed to belong to the Royals. Gregor Blanco hit a leadoff single and alertly sped to second on a long fly ball before scoring on Pablo Sandoval's double. Buster Posey was thrown out at home on the play, but Hunter Pence picked up Posey and third-base coach Tim Flannery immediately, lining a two-run homer to center. A crowd that had roared for an hour leading up to the first inning looked on in silence as Giants tore through the dugout to meet Pence at the top step. Was he aware of the sudden lack of noise?

"No, it was really loud in my head," Pence said.

Bumgarner made sure the locals would stay seated. He was tested just once, when a Brandon Crawford error

and Mike Moustakas double put two in scoring position with no outs in the third. Bumgarner takes special pride in those moments when he can pick up a teammate, and he responded with two strikeouts before loading the bases ahead of cleanup hitter Eric Hosmer, who had seen all fastballs in the first inning when he lined out to deep right.

"I had a gut feeling he would be aggressive," Bumgarner said. "So I just threw him a cutter."

Hosmer rolled it over harmlessly to second, ending the inning.

"It's what he's done all year," Crawford said. "They were getting some momentum, and he cut that off."

The Giants kept rolling in the fourth, knocking Shields out and scoring two more runs. They added

HUNTER PENCE LAUNCHES A 421-FOOT HOME RUN IN THE TOP OF THE FIRST INNING. PENCE'S BLAST GAVE THE GIANTS AN EARLY 3-0 LEAD. (JOSIE LEPE/STAFF)

two more in the seventh, running away with their seventh straight World Series win. Throughout, they made the kinds of plays that were expected from the Royals this week. The Giants spent four days hearing about Kansas City's defense and dominant bullpen and…"Speed," Crawford said, smiling as he cut a reporter off.

But it was the Giants, particularly Crawford and Blanco, who chased balls down. It was the Giants' relievers — Javier Lopez and Hunter Strickland — who breezed. It was their ace locking up his "big game" reputation.

In the third World Series start of a career that keeps soaring to new heights, Bumgarner found a way to toy with the hottest team in baseball. He has a slow curveball that he tinkers with in spring training and has thrown a couple of dozen times in games, and he threw it twice while retiring 12 straight in the heart of the game. Perez and Moustakas both got 67 mph benders.

"It's just going off the way the hitters look in their previous swing or what kind of feel I have for it," Bumgarner said. "It's just changing speeds, you know?"

Bumgarner said the pitch is meant to give hitters a different look, but his never changes. The last ace in the postseason deck was in control through the seventh and picked up his sixth postseason win, setting a franchise record.

"This is a big stage, a loud crowd, but he just keeps that maniacal focus," manager Bruce Bochy said. "He's as good as anybody I've seen at it." ∎

GIANTS PLAYERS CELEBRATE AFTER SAN FRANCISCO TOPPED KANSAS CITY TO TAKE GAME 1. (JOSE CARLOS FAJARDO/STAFF)

WORLD SERIES: GAME 2

OCTOBER 22, 2014 | ROYALS 7, GIANTS 2

GIANT MELTDOWN

ROYALS ROCK S.F. BULLPEN IN FIVE-RUN SIXTH INNING, EVEN SERIES AT ONE

BY ALEX PAVLOVIC

KANSAS CITY, MO. —The collapse was as quick as it was complete, and it left the Giants blurry, bruised and scrambling to find solutions in a series that flipped in a hurry.

A night after they romped in the World Series opener, the Giants fell 7-2 to the Kansas City Royals in a game decided by a five-run sixth inning that had five Giants toeing the rubber.

Manager Bruce Bochy was left wondering how to get the ball from his starters to the shutdown arms at the back end of his bullpen. Tim Lincecum was left lamenting the bad luck that turned his first postseason appearance into a visit to the trainer's room with lower back tightness. Hunter Strickland was asked to try to explain actions that nearly cleared the benches. The bats were left to recover after a night spent waving at sizzling fastballs from the Royals bullpen.

The Giants knew they were in for a fight in this series, but they couldn't have imagined a night like this, where they lost their composure and a resurgent pitcher along with the game. They were left looking for positives, and they found a big one. After two one-sided games in Kansas City, the series is tied heading back to San Francisco, where the Giants will host three games.

"You'd like to get greedy, but we know it's going to be a tough series," Bochy said. "It was a tight game until the sixth, but that's the way it's going to be. With their pitching and our pitching and the way both teams play, we are going to have a fight, I think, every game.

"It just got away from us there in the sixth ... but you go home, and I think you take a split."

The Giants will try to regroup and find a way to solve the issues that sunk them in the bottom of the sixth, a frame that started with the teams tied at two. Jake Peavy teetered early in the game but found his command and retired 10 straight before the inning. Lorenzo Cain ignited the rally with a leadoff single to center, and Eric Hosmer worked a tough walk. Bochy turned to his well-rested bullpen and tried to play the matchups, but it blew up in his face.

Jean Machi was called on to face Billy Butler, and it was clear that Bochy was looking for one outcome. Only four relievers induced more double plays than Machi's 12, and Butler, the plodding D.H., hit into 21 of them this season. Machi committed a cardinal sin, though, falling behind 2-0. He had to throw a strike, and Butler lined the meatball into left for a tiebreaking single.

The Giants are in the World Series in large part because of Travis Ishikawa's contributions, but his inexperience in the outfield showed as Cain steamrolled around third. Third base coach Mike Jirschele sent the speedy outfielder without hesitation and despite the fact that Ishikawa scooped the ball up with Cain still a dozen feet from reaching third. He scored easily as Ishikawa made a late throw that was cut off.

"That's his lack of experience as far as charging the ball and getting rid of it," Bochy said. "That's an area we know is not going to be our strength because this kid hasn't been out there very much."

Machi was done, and Javier Lopez retired Alex Gordon before giving way to Strickland, the hard-throwing rookie who was thought to be rehabilitated. Strickland allowed four postseason homers in advance of the World Series, but Bochy wanted to put him back in tight spots, so he had Strickland pitch the ninth inning Wednesday. It was a clean one, and Strickland got two quick strikes on Salvador Perez. But then he spiked a breaking ball that allowed both runners to advance, and threw a 97 mph fastball that caught too much of the plate. Perez slammed it into the gap in left-center for a double, scoring two as Kauffman Stadium rumbled. Omar Infante followed and lined a 98 mph fastball into the home bullpen to give the Royals a five-run lead. That's when Strickland's sour night took another ugly turn.

He had exchanged glares with Bryce Harper in the N.L. Division Series, and he thought Perez was yelling something at him as Infante rounded the bases. Strickland yelled right back, and several players started breaking out of the dugouts and bullpens.

"I assumed he was yelling at me — that's my fault for assuming," Strickland said. "I was mad at myself. I got caught up, and I didn't control my emotions like I should have. It was just a miscommunication. My emotions got the best of me. I'm not proud of that."

Perez said he was baffled by the dust-up.

"He (started) to look at me, so I asked him, 'Hey, why you look at me?'" he said. "You don't have to treat me like that. Look at Omar. Omar hit the bomb. I didn't hit the bomb. I hit a double."

The bigger problem for the Giants was Strickland's

performance. Bochy had hoped to count on Strickland and Machi for big outs against a deep Royals lineup, but both have faltered in the postseason. Lincecum looked like he might finally provide a bridge to the back end of the bullpen. He retired five straight in his first postseason appearance but was pulled after feeling tightness in his lower back. He'll be re-evaluated Thursday.

On the other side, the Royals' pen proved to be as advertised. The Giants got a leadoff homer from Gregor Blanco and an RBI double from Brandon Belt off starter Yordano Ventura, but Kelvin Herrera shut down a sixth-inning threat with 101 mph fastballs, and Wade Davis and Greg Holland struck out five in the final two innings.

"You've got your work cut out when you get five runs down," Bochy said. "That's an uphill climb against this pen."

It's one you're not going to survive this time of the year. ■

TIM LINCECUM DELIVERS HIS FINAL PITCH OF GAME 2 IN THE EIGHTH INNING. AFTER PITCHING 1 2/3 INNINGS OF SCORELESS RELIEF, LINCECUM LEFT THE GAME AFTER EXPERIENCING LOWER BACK TIGHTNESS. (JOSIE LEPE/STAFF)

HEAT IS ON

ROYALS TAKE SERIES LEAD AS DOMINANT BULLPEN CONTINUES TO SLAM DOOR ON LATE GIANTS THREATS

BY ALEX PAVLOVIC

SAN FRANCISCO—The Giants stood at their lockers late into the night after Game 3 and went back through the nitty-gritty of the individual matchups that got away in a 3-2 loss to the Royals. They talked at length about the belief that they can come back and pointed out that they have a history of doing it.

But ultimately, this World Series can now be summarized by just seven simple words.

"We're going to have to score early," Michael Morse said.

They're certainly not likely to score late against the Royals.

The best bullpen trio in baseball sealed the Royals' Game 3 win at AT&T Park and put the Giants in an unfamiliar spot. Their first World Series home loss since 2002 has them down 2-1 in the series. The franchise that took down the Rangers in five and swept the Tigers has found its toughest foe yet, an American League champion that plays National League baseball and is inspired by a much-maligned manager who jokes about being called stupid and then pushes all the right buttons.

A victorious Ned Yost took the podium after his squad's win and was asked to explain his decision to let reliever Kelvin Herrera bat with speedy Jarrod Dyson on first and two outs in the seventh inning of a one-run game. Herrera, the 101-mph throwing right-hander, had not had an at-bat since he was a 17-year-old in the Dominican Republic. Yost never wanted the at-bat to happen in the first place, but not because he was going to use a pinch-hitter.

"Actually, I was hoping (Dyson) would make an out there," Yost said. "But he steps up and foils my plan and gets a hit."

And right then and there, it was made clear that the two-time champion Giants are in for an altogether different kind of challenge as they aim for a third title. Yost's playbook this month reads: "Find some way to get a lead to Herrera, Wade Davis and Greg Holland, and then hold on until the 27th out." It's a formula the Giants haven't been able to crack.

"They're not unbeatable by any means, but these guys are pretty tough," right-hander Tim Hudson said. "They're as tough as you'll find in the game right now. Ultimately, I cost us the ballgame right there with the runs I gave up in the sixth inning."

That was when the maneuvering started in a fascinating back-and-forth between two similar teams. Hudson trailed 1-0 at that point, having been ambushed on the first World Series pitch of his career. The 39-year-old spent the days in Kansas City repeatedly turning to his three children and saying, "You realize we're in the World Series?"

"Yes, dad," they would respond. "You keep saying that."

Hudson didn't have any time to pinch himself Friday. He waited more than 3,000 innings to throw a World

Series pitch, and Alcides Escobar smoked it off the left field wall. He scored two batters later to give the Royals an early 1-0 lead.

Yost's maneuvering started before the game, when he scrambled his entire lineup to put Dyson, an excellent defender, in center field. Lorenzo Cain, one of the league's best defensive center fielders, was moved to right, bumping No. 2 hitter Nori Aoki to the bench. Yost wanted more coverage of AT&T Park's vast outfield, and Cain promptly ended the first two innings with sliding catches in right.

Hudson had a shaky second but recovered to retire 12 straight and take a one-run deficit into the sixth. As they did to Jake Peavy in the sixth inning of Game 2, the Royals knocked out Hudson before he could finish the inning.

Escobar bounced a one-out single up the middle, and Hudson elevated a fastball to Alex Gordon that was lined off the center field wall, giving the Royals a second run. Bochy called for Javier Lopez, who held left-handed hitters to a .194 average this season. Eric Hosmer fouled off six pitches before smacking the 11th pitch of the at-bat up the middle to put the Royals up by three.

"He forced me to make one more pitch, and he did what he's been doing all postseason and really squared it up," Lopez said. "I was trying to keep him off balance, but he put up a great at-bat. He really grinded."

After marinating on the 7-2 loss in Game 2 for a day, Bochy said Friday afternoon that he would adjust his late-innings plan. He used Sergio Romo for four outs and Jeremy Affeldt for four more, and the Giants inched closer. Morse's pinch double got them on the board in the sixth and brought Herrera into the game. He walked Gregor Blanco on four pitches before getting three straight groundouts. One of them, Buster Posey's bouncer to second, brought a second run home.

Yost was desperate to get the lead into the eighth and hand it over to Davis and Holland, and that meant Herrera made his major league debut as a hitter in the seventh inning of a World Series game. He practically backed into the Giants dugout while flailing at Romo's pitches, and the plan looked as though it would backfire

when Herrera walked Hunter Pence to start the bottom of the inning. But he struck out Brandon Belt on a 97 mph fastball, and rookie Brandon Finnegan got the last two outs of the seventh. Davis and Holland got the final six outs on just 20 pitches.

"It's the World Series, so it's not like you're going to face any Joe Shmoe," Morse said. "These guys are good, and they're here for a reason."

Bochy has found an unlikely match in Yost, who sticks to his guns despite what the book or numbers might say. He let two pitchers hit in the sixth and seventh innings even though that meant leaving his D.H., Billy Butler, on the bench all night.

"I didn't lose the game," Yost said. "So I don't think about that stuff."

His formula has the Royals in their first World Series in 29 years and the Giants two losses from elimination. They went home vowing to turn the tide. There seems only one way to do it.

"We've got to make sure we do what we did in the first game," hitting coach Hensley Meulens said. "Score early so we don't see them." ■

BUSTER POSEY REACTS AFTER FLYING OUT TO LEFT FIELD TO LEAD OFF THE NINTH INNING. THE GIANTS' NO. 3 HITTER WAS HITLESS IN FOUR AT-BATS. (JOSIE LEPE/STAFF)

BACK TO EVEN

GIANTS SHRUG OFF AN EARLY DEFICIT TO POUND ROYALS

By Alex Pavlovic

SAN FRANCISCO—It was a four-hour epic with twists and turns that were mostly whipped away by the driving wind by the time the Giants shook hands at the pitcher's mound and grinned about their new reality.

On a night that started so poorly, the Giants rallied to rout the Kansas City Royals 11-4 Saturday and put a tied World Series on the left arm of Madison Bumgarner, this postseason's biggest star and the Game 5 starter.

The clubhouse brimmed with standouts, but the glue throughout was a 29-year-old journeyman pitching in October for the first time. This night was bigger than that for Yusmeiro Petit, though.

His father, Alberto, tackled his fear of flying to travel from Venezuela to San Francisco and watch his son pitch in the big leagues for the first time. Yusmeiro went out and pitched three brilliant innings in the middle of the madness, stabilizing the Giants until the lineup could recover and assure that the Royals couldn't turn to their unbeatable back of the bullpen.

"We had to win this game tonight no matter what," said starter Ryan Vogelsong, who didn't make it out of the third. "The shift came when Petit came in and slammed the door shut and let the lineup go to work. We needed to tie this series and get the ball to Madison."

As Bumgarner quietly walked out of the park late Saturday night, his mind already churning, Petit stood on the damp infield at AT&T Park and gathered his family for a photo. He smiled wide as he hugged relatives who carried paper bags full of Giants gear. Hours earlier, he had allowed a park filled with that same orange and black to finally take a deep breath.

The Giants scored first Saturday but were down by three after the top of the third. It could have been much worse or much better. The inches went against Vogelsong, but the Giants managed to keep the game from spiraling after the bases had been loaded.

Vogelsong needed just 28 pitches to get through the first two innings, 23 of them strikes. He felt locked in and felt he had great stuff.

"This is the first time I can remember being on the mound with all four pitches working in a while," he said later, shaking his head.

Play the third inning 10 times and Vogelsong probably gets out of it cleanly in nine, but a series of misplays sent him back to the clubhouse, where, as is his tradition, he sat quietly in a leather chair and watched the rest of the game. With a runner on and one out, Alex Gordon hit a grounder to first, but the Giants were a beat slow on the double-play try. Gordon stole second, and Lorenzo Cain followed with an infield single on a slow roller to short. Eric Hosmer made weak contact, too, but his roller to the right side was just out of the reach of Vogelsong. Brandon Belt went far off the bag to field it and threw back to Vogelsong, who was out of

BUSTER POSEY SCORES ON PABLO SANDOVAL'S SIXTH-INNING SINGLE. SANDOVAL'S CLUTCH HIT BROKE A 4-4 TIE. (NHAT V. MEYER/STAFF)

position. Hosmer got his foot to the bag first. Vogelsong steamed as he watched Gordon race across the plate.

"Everything kind of went wrong on that pitch," he said.

In the dugout, manager Bruce Bochy took off his cap and swiped at a dugout railing.

"It was frustration because he was making good pitches," Bochy said. "I just felt for him. I mean, this guy was making great pitches and we couldn't get that last out. I think if he gets out of that inning, he throws a nice game for us."

Vogelsong would end up throwing only 14 more pitches. Omar Infante ripped one of them, an elevated cutter, up the middle to score two runs. Salvador Perez put the Royals up 4-1 with a broken-bat flare to center.

Vogelsong had not had a chance to hit yet, so when Bochy went to his bullpen, he chose struggling right-hander Jean Machi instead of Petit. Bochy was hopeful Machi could get the final out and give way to a pinch-hitter. He walked the bases loaded and went to a full count on opposing pitcher Jason Vargas before finally ending an inning that lasted half an hour.

The Giants got a run back in bottom of the third and kept rolling in the fifth. Joe Panik's leadoff double knocked Vargas out of the game, and Hunter Pence drove him in. With one out and Pence on, the Royals called on Danny Duffy to give Pablo Sandoval, a .199 hitter against lefties this season, a tougher matchup. Sandoval was so flu-ridden that he required an IV before the game and skipped fielding drills, but he lashed a single up the middle to send Pence to third. He scored on a sacrifice fly by Juan Perez.

Petit had thrown two scoreless innings to that point — and picked up his sixth hit in 106 career at-bats —

and he cruised through the top of the sixth, continuing his run as the unlikely duplicator of Tim Lincecum's 2012 postseason. Lincecum pitched 13 innings out of the bullpen during that title run, giving up three hits and one run. Petit has allowed just four hits in his dozen scoreless innings.

"We're fortunate to have a guy like this that we can call on when things don't go right," Bochy said. "He does calm things down."

The Giants would ramp it up again in the bottom of the sixth, making a World Series winner of Petit. Joaquin Arias led off with a single, and Gregor Blanco — after failing to get a bunt down — lofted a hit into left. With two outs and the bases loaded, Sandoval got a first-pitch fastball from the left-handed Brandon Finnegan and shot it up the middle, scoring two. Belt padded the lead with an RBI single.

"It started to get contagious," Belt said.

The lead kept Kansas City's big three relievers of Kelvin Herrera, Wade Davis and Greg Holland sidelined, and the Giants pounded the soft spot in the Royals bullpen. They added four more runs in the bottom of the seventh to pull away and even the series. The Giants and Royals have thrown everything at each other for four nights. The series is best-of-three now.

"This is the biggest stage, and to have two teams laying it all on the line, that's the ultimate in sports," Pence said. "We're in the World Series, and we have two teams that are competing as fierce as you'll ever see. That's a lot of fun." ■

HUNTER PENCE SCORES ON BRANDON BELT'S SIXTH-INNING SINGLE TO GIVE THE GIANTS A 7-4 LEAD. PENCE CONTRIBUTED THREE HITS AS THE GIANTS EVENED THE SERIES AT 2-2. (NHAT V. MEYER/STAFF)

WORLD SERIES: GAME 5

OCTOBER 26, 2014 | GIANTS 5, ROYALS 0

WITHIN REACH

BUMGARNER'S GAME 5 MASTERPIECE PUTS GIANTS ONE WIN AWAY

BY ALEX PAVLOVIC

SAN FRANCISCO—Madison Bumgarner has been in complete command of this postseason, etching his long name in the record books with one of the most dominant months in MLB history.

He looks unbothered as he overpowers lineups on the sport's biggest stage, like he's pitching on a Tuesday in June, his teammates say. But Bumgarner, for all his poise and precociousness, is not above having a superstitious streak.

Long before the Giants' 5-0 win over the Kansas City Royals in Game 5 of the World Series, Bumgarner stood quietly in a corner of the AT&T Park clubhouse, lost amid a celebration of the Giants' clinch of a playoff spot. He poured three Bud Light cans into his mouth at once. After a wild-card win, it was two cans and two bottles. The celebratory chug — a word used liberally since most of the suds end up on his shirt — was upped to five beers after the NLDS and six when Bumgarner, the NLCS MVP, put the Giants back in the World Series.

His otherworldly performance Sunday put Bumgarner on the verge of the seven-beer celebration he has chased all month, and it has the Giants 27 outs from a third title in five years.

Twenty-five days after he started this postseason run with a four-hit shutout of the Pirates, Bumgarner bookended his October résumé with the first World Series shutout since the Marlins' Josh Beckett did it in 2003.

He again allowed just four hits while becoming the first pitcher in MLB history to throw a World Series shutout with no walks and at least eight strikeouts. Bumgarner lowered his ERA in four career World Series starts to a record 0.29, and his mark in six starts this postseason dropped to 1.13. His most impressive statistic is one that rises by the quick inning. Bumgarner has thrown $47\frac{2}{3}$ innings in 26 days, the second-biggest workload in postseason history.

"I felt great. I felt great all night," he said. "This time of the year, it's not too hard to go out there and feel good."

Thanks to Bumgarner, the surefire Series MVP if the Giants win one more game, an organization woke up Monday morning knowing it's one more win away from fully forming a dynasty.

"There is definitely a different feeling," catcher Buster Posey said. "From the moment you wake up, you have a different feeling. It's special. It's a special feeling. Hopefully it's something we all embrace and enjoy."

Bumgarner seems not to notice it, at least during his starts. As he mowed down the Royals in a ballpark that shook and chanted "M-V-P" repeatedly, Bumgarner wore an expression of peace. There was no emphatic double-fist pump after his 117th and final pitch, just a quick handshake and hug with Posey. As Bumgarner worked toward a startlingly easy shutout, teammates noted no

MADISON BUMGARNER DELIVERS THE 117TH AND FINAL PITCH OF GAME 5. THE GIANTS' ACE PITCHED A 4-HIT SHUTOUT AS THE GIANTS TOOK A 3-2 SERIES LEAD. (D. ROSS CAMERON/STAFF)

change in his demeanor. Shortstop Brandon Crawford saw Bumgarner joking around in the dugout after one dominant inning.

"No big deal — just hanging out here with a shutout in Game 5 of the World Series, " Crawford said later, smiling.

The mastery started when the game did. Bumgarner struck out four in the first two innings and retired 10 straight at one point. The Giants rewarded him with two early runs, one with what has become their trademark manufactured style. Hunter Pence led off the second with a single, and Brandon Belt stunned teammates and the Royals with a perfect bunt that beat a shift. Belt had never bunted for a hit in a big league game. He made the decision a split-second before James Shields delivered a cutter.

"I figured that was a good time to do it," he said. "If it didn't work out, we still have a runner in scoring position with good hitters coming up."

Travis Ishikawa fell behind in the count but skied a ball deep enough to center that both runners tagged and advanced. Pence scored when Crawford bounced a two-strike pitch to second. The run was the Giants' 18th of the postseason that was scored on something other than a hit.

The Giants scored a more conventional run in the fourth. Pablo Sandoval singled and Ishikawa moved him up with a hard grounder that stayed down in the dirt and got just under shortstop Alcides Escobar's glove. Crawford again fell behind to Shields, who was much improved from Game 1, but he stayed back on a diving curveball and chipped it into center. Sandoval rumbled home when Jarrod Dyson bobbled the ball.

"That was not one of my best swings, but I'll take it," Crawford said.

He would add a third RBI in the eighth as the Giants tacked on three more. The big hit was a two-run double from Juan Perez, who came inches away from becoming the first hitter all year to take Wade Davis deep. Perez had spent much of the night trying to compose himself after learning mid-game of the tragic death of 22-year-old Cardinals outfielder Oscar Taveras. Perez had known Taveras since 2009 and his family much longer, and he had tears in his eyes as he talked of Taveras being a "humble, happy and good kid."

When the throw from center went to the plate, Perez broke for third and slid in headfirst with a cloud of dust. He pointed at the dugout and screamed, "Let's go!" Then he pointed to the sky.

"That was for you," he said to Taveras.

Manager Bruce Bochy had closer Santiago Casilla up in the eighth, but even with the game broken open, he stuck with Bumgarner. For long stretches, it had seemed almost unfair to ask hitters to face the challenge. No at-bat exemplified that more than Lorenzo Cain's ground out in the fourth.

Bumgarner got two quick strikes with an 86 mph slider and 75 mph curveball. He dropped the curve down to 65 mph but missed. After Cain fouled off a 92 mph fastball, Bumgarner dialed it back down to 76 with a curveball that Cain harmlessly bounced to short.

"This guy was right on tonight," Bochy said. "He was strong all night. When this guy is on, it's fun to watch."

It can also be remarkably stress-free for men playing in the World Series.

"He doesn't give you a whole lot of work to do," Belt said. "He never lets the moment get too big for him. To be only 25 years old and do that, that's pretty special."

Just about every inning of his long month has been. Bumgarner and Curt Schilling are the only pitchers in MLB history to throw at least seven innings in six starts in one postseason, and Bumgarner might not be done. He said he feels strong enough to come out of the bullpen if the series goes seven. How many pitches can he throw?

"I'm not a big pitch count guy," he said.

Turns out he keeps close count only during celebrations, and he's one step closer to the final one. ∎

PABLO SANDOVAL HEADS HOME TO SCORE ON JUAN PEREZ'S EIGHTH-INNING DOUBLE. (D. ROSS CAMERON/STAFF)

WORLD SERIES: GAME 6
OCTOBER 28, 2014 | ROYALS 10, GIANTS O

ROUTED TO GAME 7

GIANTS TAKE ROUGH ROAD TO DECIDING CONTEST
AS ROYALS CRUISE TO LOPSIDED VICTORY

BY ALEX PAVLOVIC

KANSAS CITY, MO.—It took just 3 hours, 21 minutes for the Giants to get blown out of Kauffman Stadium on in Game 6. They didn't need much longer to shift gears into underdog mode.

After a 10-0 loss to the Kansas City Royals, manager Bruce Bochy embraced the fact that the home team has won Game 7 of the World Series nine straight times. He'll likely address the team Wednesday night, and he already knows what he wants to say.

"They're going against the odds — we've done that before," Bochy said. "You go back to 2012 and look at this postseason. I think a lot of people had us getting beat in the first and second round. This club is so resilient. They're so tough. They'll put this behind them."

Bochy did it as Jake Peavy walked quickly back to the clubhouse at the end of the second inning, glove in hand, a pained look on his face and a seven-run deficit on the scoreboard. It's all hands on deck in Game 7, but that meant some key hands had to stay clean in Game 6. Bochy got just four outs from Peavy, so he turned to Jean Machi for a career-high 51 pitches. Hunter Strickland threw two innings for the first time since having Tommy John surgery. Ryan Vogelsong made his first relief appearance since 2011. Buster Posey was the first starter to hit the bench, and others followed.

The Giants got as much rest as they could as Kauffman Stadium turned the penultimate game of the season into a party. As the Royals circled the bases and their 23-year-old right-hander, Yordano Ventura, blossomed from tantalizing talent to star, the Giants started to embrace all that a Game 7 means. This is just the sixth one in the past 26 World Series.

"A Game 7 in a World Series is a gift for everyone," Hunter Pence said, smiling. "It's pretty special. It's incredibly entertaining for fans and incredibly entertaining for the world and the game of baseball. It's incredibly fun to play in and compete in."

To guarantee a dynasty instead of disappointment, the Giants will need to be far more competitive than they were Tuesday. Bochy was able to make so many rare moves because this one was over after the top of the third.

The trouble actually started two innings earlier, when Peavy gave up a walk and hard-hit ball to left. The Royals failed to score when Lorenzo Cain missed third-base coach Mike Jirschele's send and held up as Travis Ishikawa, who had slipped, threw the ball back into second instead of toward the plate. Cain's lapse would be forgotten an inning later.

The Royals set franchise postseason records with eight hits and seven runs in the 33-minute second inning, and they did damage off both Peavy and long man Yusmeiro Petit, who had previously been perfect in the postseason. The nightmare frame started innocently enough, with a broken-bat single by Alex Gordon. Salvador Perez followed with a rocket to right-center, and Petit immediately got up in the bullpen. Mike Moustakas hit a bouncer just inside the first base line that was a couple of inches away from a diving Brandon Belt's glove and went for an RBI double. At that point, Javier Lopez joined Petit on the bullpen mound. The late-innings lefty would sit down soon enough as the game quickly got out of hand. Alcides Escobar hit a hard grounder to first, and Belt moved toward home, ready to throw Perez out. But the catcher stayed at third, and when Belt turned back toward first, he didn't have enough time to beat the speedy Escobar to the bag.

"I saw him break for home, and that's when I made the move," Belt said. "He just kind of stopped. He did his job right there. It was just a weird play."

With the bases now loaded, Nori Aoki fouled off four pitches before lining a single into left.

That was it for Peavy, who has a 7.98 career ERA in the postseason and has allowed nine runs in 6⅓ innings this series. His catcher felt he deserved much better.

"I thought that was as crisp as I've seen him this postseason," Posey said. "They were able to get the bat on some tough pitches and make things happen."

Peavy gave up six hits, but only one went for extra bases. In a strange way, he said, it would have been better to constantly be turning and watching balls leave the yard.

"It's almost easier if you go out there and take a beating," he said. "This was hugely disappointing. The only thing you can do other than strike guys out is hope they make contact and you're able to defend it. You're excited (Eric) Hosmer and Cain and Alex Gordon hit the ball the way they hit it. It takes some good fortune — a ball right at somebody. That wasn't the case tonight."

Petit hasn't needed any serendipity this month. He gave up just four hits to the 42 batters he faced before Tuesday, but the Royals welcomed him with three straight hits. Bochy tries to save Petit for the start of innings, but he had little choice but to use him in a bases-loaded jam and hope for some more of that October magic. It had taken the night off.

Cain was Petit's first batter, and he hit a single to center that scored two. The Giants pulled the infield in for Hosmer, and he bounced a ball off the dirt in front of the plate and over shortstop Brandon Crawford. Hosmer hustled for a double as two more runs scored. Billy Butler scorched a double that made it 7-0.

The Giants briefly flirted with a comeback. Ventura went nearly 40 minutes between pitches, and he walked the bases loaded ahead of Posey in the top half of the third. Posey hit into a double play on the first pitch. The missed opportunity meant Petit would be saved for Game 7. Ditto for the rest of Bochy's regular relievers. Posey finally got a breather after catching the first 149 innings of the postseason.

"You hate to have a game go like this, but no question it does allow you to do some things you probably normally wouldn't," Bochy said. "So we're loaded tomorrow, I feel, and they are, too."

That was thanks to Ventura, who wore Oscar Taveras' initials on his blue cap and later said the game was dedicated to the 22-year-old Cardinals player who died as the result of a car crash Sunday. Ventura and his 100 mph fastball allowed just three hits in seven innings.

"That's one of the best arms you'll see in the game," Pence said.

The Giants won't see it Wednesday, but just about everyone else on both sides will be available. That includes Madison Bumgarner and Royals ace James Shields. The numbers say the Giants are in for a tough task. The road team hasn't taken Game 7 since 1979.

"Listen, this bunch doesn't care," Peavy said. "We'll show up tomorrow and find any which way to win." ∎

A FAMILIAR RING

GIANTS RIDE BUMGARNER TO FINISH LINE, CAPTURE THIRD TITLE IN FIVE SEASONS

BY ALEX PAVLOVIC

KANSAS CITY, MO.—It was their rallying cry in good times and in bad, a joyous chorus picked up by Hunter Pence while watching a college football game. The Giants used it to celebrate homers, fire up the fan base on the eve of the postseason and check off one clinch after the next during a stirring October run.

On Wednesday, the cheer served as a summary of baseball's latest dynasty.

Champions in 2010? Yes. Champions in 2012? Yes. Champions in 2014? Yes.

Madison Bumgarner threw the Giants' first pitch of the World Series and the last, a fastball that was popped up with the tying run on third. When it settled into third baseman Pablo Sandoval's glove, the Giants had a 3-2 win over the Kansas City Royals in a wildly entertaining Game 7 and a permanent place in the game's history books. They are the first franchise to win three titles in five years since the Yankees of the late 1990s, and the first National League franchise to have such a dominant stretch since the Cardinals of the 1940s.

Over three postseasons, with three vastly different casts, the Giants proved unbeatable. They have won 10 consecutive postseason series, a streak that spelled dynasty in a clubhouse soaked by cheap beer and Mumm champagne.

"In today's game, if it's not (a dynasty), it's as close as you're going to get," catcher Buster Posey said.

Posey rushed to meet Bumgarner as the ball settled into Sandoval's glove. As the bullpen emptied and the dugout rushed for the mound, the two superstars, the 27-year-old catcher and the 25-year-old left-hander, shared a hug. After the postseason the Giants just went through, they might have been holding each other up as much as celebrating.

Posey caught every inning but two of the championship run, including every pitch of Bumgarner's record $52\frac{2}{3}$ innings. Bumgarner pitched 21 innings in the series, earning two wins and a five-inning save. He never flinched, but when it was over and Bumgarner was MVP of the World Series, as well as of the NLCS, the facade broke.

"You know what, I can't lie to you anymore," he said. "I'm a little tired now."

Deep in their eyes, the Giants all looked a little worn down Wednesday night. They are the first team to start a postseason with a wild-card game and finish it with a parade. The procession kicked off shortly after Wednesday's game, when manager Bruce Bochy walked the 20-pound World Series trophy into the center of the clubhouse. His eyes red, he looked at a group that willed itself to a title nobody else saw coming.

"I'm numb through all of this," Bochy said, smiling and shaking his head. "This group of warriors continues to amaze me. Nobody wanted it more than them."

That was true when the Giants jumped out to the

MADISON BUMGARNER (LEFT) CELEBRATES WITH BUSTER POSEY AFTER THE FINAL OUT OF GAME 7. BUMGARNER EARNED WORLD SERIES MVP HONORS AFTER WINNING GAME 1 AND GAME 5 AND PITCHING FIVE INNINGS OF SCORELESS RELIEF IN GAME 7. (JOSE CARLOS FAJARDO/STAFF)

best record of baseball through the season's first two months, and when they fell flat as the summer wore on. There was an unshakable faith, and when it wavered, the Giants reminded one another of who they were.

"Through all the tough times, we said, 'Don't forget: We're the best team in the world,'" Pence said. "You've got to believe it."

Bochy sent the message one last time in the minutes before the first pitch. The road team had lost Game 7 nine straight times, but Bochy gathered his players and reminded them that they won the wild-card game in Pittsburgh. They took the first game of the NLDS in Washington, D.C., and the opener of the NLCS in St. Louis. After the speech, Bochy got to work, and he had one of his busiest nights as a manager. The Royals' Ned Yost did, too.

For the first time in a Game 7, neither starter would record more than 10 outs, and both bullpens warmed up starting with the second inning. The Giants struck first, loading the bases in the top of the second and scoring on sacrifice flies by Michael Morse and Brandon Crawford. The lead wouldn't last long.

Tim Hudson waited 16 years for his first World Series and Wednesday — at 39 years, 107 days — he became the oldest pitcher to ever start a Game 7 in the World Series. The biggest start of his career lasted just 42 minutes.

Hudson's pitches flattened out in the second, and the Royals quickly took advantage. Billy Butler opened with a single up the middle and rumbled home on Alex Gordon's double to right-center. When Salvador Perez was hit just above the knee, Jeremy Affeldt and Tim Lincecum started scrambling in the visitor's bullpen. Gordon scored on a sacrifice fly, and Hudson was knocked out by Alcides Escobar's single. A night after Jake Peavy got just four outs, Hudson recorded five, but the Giants were ready.

Bochy called Affeldt into his office before the game and told the late-innings left-hander to have his knee brace on from the first pitch and to stretch when Hudson took the mound. The Giants hoped to get a long night from Hudson, but if he couldn't last, Affeldt was to provide a bridge to Bumgarner. Affeldt gave up one hit over 2⅓ innings, lowering his career postseason ERA to 0.86 and extending his scoreless outings streak to 22 games, one shy of Mariano Rivera's postseason record.

"He saved us," Ryan Vogelsong said. "He absolutely saved us."

As Vogelsong watched Affeldt set the Royals down, he noticed that Bumgarner was starting to stir. The left-hander watched the end of one inning from the edge of the dugout, his long fingers wrapped around a chain-link fence, his toes inches from the warning track. The Giants wanted desperately to get a lead in Bumgarner's hands, and Morse and Joe Panik assured that they would. With a runner on and no outs in the third, the rookie second baseman dived headlong for a grounder and glove-flipped it to Crawford, who completed a double play. Panik, a converted shortstop, has never even worked on that particular play.

"I've never ever done that," he said. "There wasn't enough time to think about anything. It was just instincts taking over."

Brute strength took over an inning later, getting the Giants the last run they would need in 2014. Singles by Sandoval and Pence brought Kelvin Herrera, usually a seventh-inning reliever, into the fourth. He threw a two-strike 99 mph fastball in on Morse's hands, but the 6-foot-5 slugger nicknamed "The Beast" was strong enough to fist it into right field, giving the Giants the lead.

Bumgarner had only two days to rest after a 117-pitch shutout, and he didn't waste many bullets in the bullpen, throwing just enough warm-up pitches to get his arm slot into place. The staff's ace sauntered slowly out of the bullpen at the start of the fifth, jogging to the infield and then walking the rest of the way.

GIANTS SHORTSTOP BRANDON CRAWFORD LEAPS TO AVOID ALEX GORDON'S SLIDE TO COMPLETE A DOUBLE PLAY IN THE FOURTH INNING. (D. ROSS CAMERON/STAFF)

"As soon as I saw him warming up and we had the lead, I knew it was over," Hudson said. "I knew the big fella was going to get it done."

For four innings, it was that simple. Bumgarner gave up a leadoff single but then retired 14 straight. Before the game, pitching coach Dave Righetti had told Bochy that Bumgarner was good for 50-70 pitches. Trainer Dave Groeschner wasn't concerned as the ninth approached.

"He's so strong, and he willed himself through this," Groeschner said. "He's special."

Righetti has long known that, but he checked on Bumgarner, just in case. As closer Santiago Casilla warmed up for the bottom of the ninth, Righetti looked over at Bumgarner in the dugout. It was hard to tell if he had a pulse. Bumgarner looked up and nodded. The ninth was his.

After two quick outs, Gordon hit a liner to center that Gregor Blanco considered diving for. He backed off and the ball skipped past him and toward the wall. Blanco's heart sank. He thought Gordon would circle the bases to tie the game, but he held up at third. Bumgarner had carried the Giants so far that it was only fitting that he picked up a teammate one more time. He got Perez to pop up, setting off the celebration and capping one of the great postseasons any player in any sport has ever had.

"He's amazing, he really is," said Hudson, a champion for the first time after 16 seasons. "He's going to go down as one of the best to ever play the game."

These Giants have permanently etched their names into the record books. Sandoval set a postseason record with 26 hits. Posey has a third title on a résumé that could put him in the Hall of Fame. If he gets there, he'll join Bochy. Nine previous managers had won three titles. All are enshrined in Cooperstown.

Bochy just smiled when asked if he's leading a dynasty, saying that's for others to decide. A few feet away, Matt Cain, the longest-tenured Giant, took in a third celebration.

"I don't know if we are, but this is a lot of fun," he said. "I hope we keep doing it." ■

MADISON BUMGARNER DELIVERS IN THE SIXTH INNING. THE GIANTS' ACE EARNED THE LONGEST SAVE IN WORLD SERIES HISTORY, PITCHING FIVE INNINGS IN GAME 7. (JOSIE LEPE/STAFF)

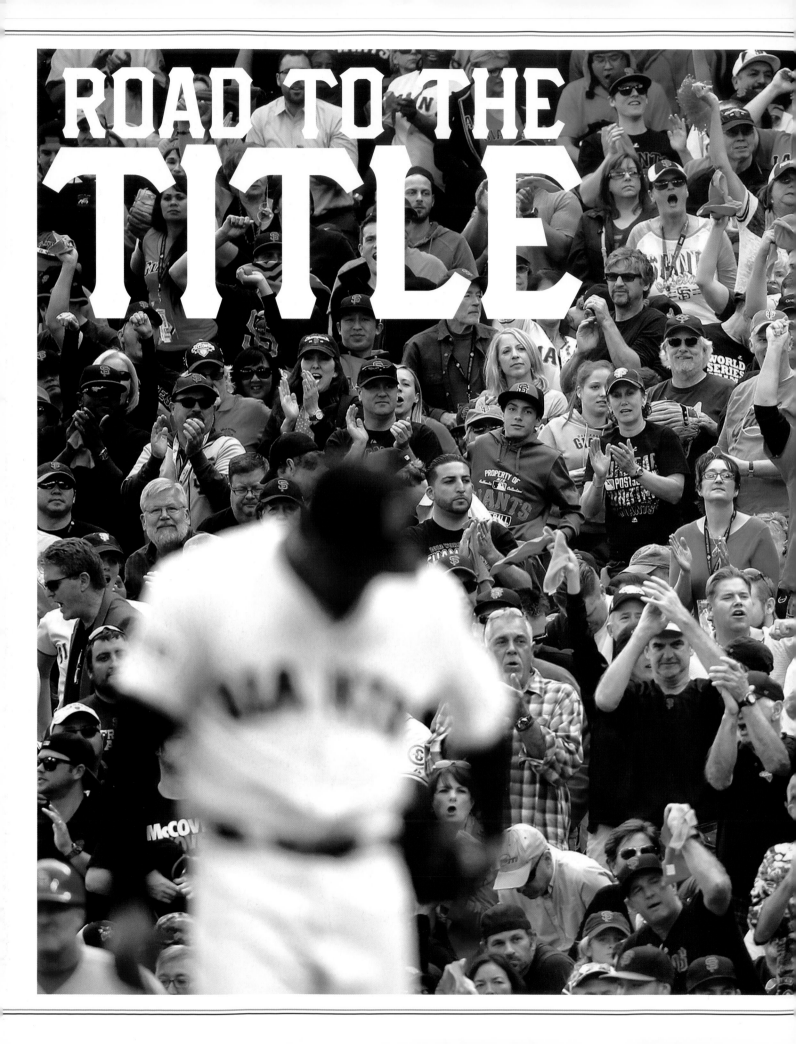

ROAD TO THE
TITLE

GIANTS FANS CHEER ON
SANTIAGO CASILLA AS THE
RELIEVER PREPARES TO FACE
THE FINAL BATTER OF THE NINTH
INNING OF GAME 3 OF THE
NLCS. THE GIANTS WON GAME
3 IN THE BOTTOM OF THE 10TH
INNING. (JOSIE LEPE/STAFF)

FREAK SHOW II

LINCECUM'S GEM AGAINST PADRES CEMENTS SPOT IN S.F. RECORD BOOK

BY ALEX PAVLOVIC ✦ JUNE 25, 2014

SAN FRANCISCO—With his whirling delivery, whipping hair and occasional mustache, Tim Lincecum might be the most distinctive star in Giants history. Now he stands alone in the franchise's record book.

Lincecum no-hit the San Diego Padres for the second time in less than a year on June 25, becoming the first player in the Giants' San Francisco era to throw multiple no-hitters. Just 347 days after a grueling 148-pitch night at Petco Park, Lincecum needed only 113 to clinch a 4-0 victory that, history aside, was desperately needed by the slumping Giants.

The no-hitter was the 16th by a Giants pitcher. Only Lincecum and Hall-of-Famer Christy Mathewson (1901, 1905) have thrown more than one. Ten days after his 30th birthday, Lincecum owns two World Series rings, two Cy Young Awards and two no-hitters. The list to have pulled that off is just as short, and just as impressive. Only Lincecum and Sandy Koufax have such a résumé.

"Right now, I guess it's really cool," Lincecum said. "When I get older, I'll be able to reflect on it a little bit more and take it for what it's worth. Right now, I'm still kind of just in the moment."

That moment was another brilliant one. Lincecum had all four pitches working on a foggy day at AT&T Park, flummoxing the light-hitting Padres, dazzling a sellout crowd and lifting teammates while allowing just a second-inning walk and striking out six. As if sensing the gravity of the moment, Lincecum added two hits, doubling his previous season total.

"It was the Tim Lincecum show," manager Bruce Bochy said. "He had such great focus. He really was an artist out there. It's hard enough to do one (no-hitter). To do two, that puts you in a different class."

The first was one of Bochy's most stressful nights as a manager. With Lincecum seemingly headed for 150 pitches last July 13, Bochy had the bullpen humming from the sixth inning on. This time the relievers were spectators, left with nothing to do but marvel at Lincecum's efficiency and command of a slider he threw 40 times to record 13 outs. When it was over, Bochy raised a clubhouse toast to Lincecum, who wore a Team USA soccer jersey and gladiator helmet.

"I just want to thank him for making this one a lot less stressful," Bochy said. "This was a lot easier."

Seemingly every no-hitter has a play that stands out, a moment when the ballpark stands still, ready to groan as one or march onward toward history. The Giants are the first team since the 1970s Angels to have a no-hitter in three straight seasons, and the previous two had their share of drama. Gregor Blanco's diving catch saved Matt Cain's perfect game in 2012. Hunter Pence's Superman

TIM LINCECUM AND CATCHER HECTOR SANCHEZ CELEBRATE AFTER LINCECUM PITCHED HIS SECOND CAREER NO-HITTER AS THE GIANTS BEAT THE SAN DIEGO PADRES 4-0 ON JUNE 25. LINCECUM JOINED CHRISTY MATHEWSON AS THE ONLY GIANTS PITCHERS TO THROW MULTIPLE NO-HITTERS. (JOHN GREEN/STAFF)

sprawl kept Lincecum's first no-hitter alive. In a joyous clubhouse Wednesday, one celebrating a win for just the third time in 11 games, no one could remember a moment of doubt.

"Every ball was hit right at us," Pence said. "There were just a couple of balls hit hard, but they were right at us. He was dominating and magnificent. It was a special performance."

Without highlights to parse, teammates instead recalled the moment they sensed the dugout was starting to tingle. Pence noticed an uptick in Lincecum's demeanor just before first pitch, when customized Team USA jerseys arrived for the two soccer fans. Bochy noted Lincecum's early focus, long a problem for a right-hander who entered with a 4.90 ERA. The manager started thinking about a no-hitter in the third inning.

"It just looked like he was putting very, very little effort into his delivery," Bochy said.

Buster Posey was behind the plate for Lincecum's other no-hitter but played first base Wednesday, contributing four hits to help pad Lincecum's lead. From the fifth inning on, Posey was on high alert. Lincecum's personal catcher, 24-year-old Hector Sanchez, tried to stay focused amid standing ovations that started after the sixth inning.

Not surprisingly, the lighthearted Lincecum never got caught up in the moment. When there was a pitching change with Lincecum on second base in the seventh, he jogged to the dugout, fist-bumping reliever Juan Gutierrez on the way in and conferring with third-base coach Tim Flannery on the way out. Lincecum chatted with teammates throughout the final three innings, laughing and mimicking his own running form at one point.

"It's almost like he's immune to the big moments," Pence said. "He's free when it's happening. He doesn't make a bigger deal out of it than it is."

Lincecum had a more simple explanation for breaking with baseball tradition, which calls for a pitcher to be left alone when flirting with history.

"I figure it's more awkward when they don't talk to you than when they do," he said.

There have been plenty of awkward nights on the mound for Lincecum in recent years, as he has struggled to find consistency with diminished stuff. On Wednesday, that wasn't a problem.

"I didn't feel my stuff was great," he said. "But the more it was down, the more movement I had. I didn't feel like it was a stuff day, it felt more like a location day."

Lincecum dotted his spots in the late innings, getting two grounders and a fly ball in the seventh, and then a grounder, fly ball and pop-up in the eighth. He jogged out in the ninth to a thundering ovation and quickly struck out pinch-hitter Chris Denorfia before getting pinch-hitter Yasmani Grandal to ground out. The 27th out came on Will Venable's soft grounder to rookie second baseman Joe Panik.

In the winning clubhouse, teammates toasted a sports-drink-soaked Lincecum for his rare achievements. He is the 32nd pitcher in MLB history to throw multiple no-hitters and the first since Addie Joss in 1910 to throw a second against one team. How would Lincecum celebrate?

"I'm going to go to my house and drink a little bit," he said, smiling. "Can I say that?"

When you have two rings, two Cy Young trophies and two no-hitters, nobody is going to stop you. ■

TIM LINCECUM DELIVERS A PITCH DURING HIS JUNE 25 NO-HITTER. THE GIANTS' VETERAN NOW OWNS THREE WORLD SERIES RINGS, TWO CY YOUNG AWARDS AND TWO NO-HITTERS. (JOHN GREEN/STAFF)

CAIN LOST FOR THE SEASON

PITCHER HAS BONE CHIPS REMOVED FROM ELBOW

By Daniel Brown ✦ August 12, 2014

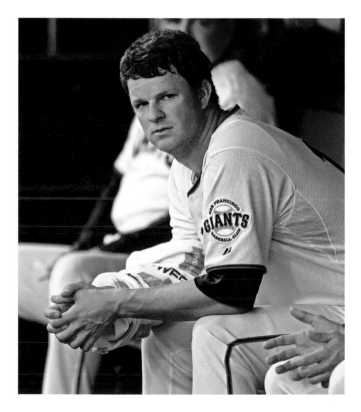

SAN FRANCISCO—Matt Cain's right elbow surgery went well, manager Bruce Bochy said Tuesday. The projected timetable for the pitcher's recovery remains at three months, which would put him on track for spring training.

Bochy knows that the bone chips came out — because he saw them himself. A jar full of the rattling debris made its way into the Giants clubhouse.

"They're pretty big. It's amazing this guy was pitching," Bochy said before the Giants took on the Chicago White Sox at AT&T Park.

Dr. Ken Akizuki, the Giants' orthopedist, performed the season-ending surgery on August 11. Besides removing the bone chips, Akizuki also "cleaned up" some bone spurs, according to Bochy.

Cain, 29, struggled to find his form this season while pitching through the injury. He was 2-7 with a 4.18 ERA before going on the disabled list retroactive to July 11.

Cain was at the game Tuesday, and Bochy said: "He's very upbeat. I think he's excited that he's gotten his elbow cleaned out." ■

OPPOSITE: MATT CAIN PITCHES AGAINST THE CINCINNATI REDS ON JUNE 28, 2014. CAIN WAS 2-7 IN 15 STARTS BEFORE HIS 2014 SEASON ENDED IN JULY. (JOSE CARLOS FAJARDO/STAFF) ABOVE: CAIN LOOKS ON FROM THE DUGOUT DURING A JUNE START. THE RIGHT-HANDER HAS 95 WINS OVER 10 SEASONS. (JOSE CARLOS FAJARDO/STAFF)

YUSMEIRO PETIT PITCHES AGAINST THE COLORADO ROCKIES IN THE FIRST INNING ON AUG. 28. HIS EIGHTH OUT OF THE GAME MARKED HIS 46TH CONSECUTIVE BATTER RETIRED, BREAKING MARK BUEHRLE'S MAJOR LEAGUE RECORD. (DAN HONDA/STAFF)

ANOTHER SHOT AT HISTORY

PETIT PUTS NAME IN RECORD BOOK

By Alex Pavlovic ✦ August 29, 2014

SAN FRANCISCO—It has been nearly a year since Yusmeiro Petit came within a strike of becoming the 24th pitcher in major league history to throw a perfect game. In the aftermath of that disappointment, Petit didn't pout or wonder why the baseball gods held him back. He simply expressed gratitude for the opportunity to have such a magical night.

The game rewarded that faith, and now Petit stands alone in the record book. His eighth out in Thursday's 4-1 win over the Colorado Rockies was his 46th straight overall, breaking Mark Buehrle's MLB record.

Petit doesn't have a perfect game on his résumé, but this feat might be even better. Over two starts and six relief appearances from July 22 through August 28, Petit pitched the equivalent of a perfect game plus 19 additional outs. He took the mound at AT&T Park with 38 straight already in the books, and thought briefly of Arizona pinch hitter Eric Chavez's single that just barely eluded right fielder Hunter Pence last Sept. 6.

"This is not going to happen to me again," Petit said as he stood on the mound.

Petit felt more relaxed this time around, even though he had five days to think about another shot at history. He has been dominant for a month, but it wasn't until a 4⅓-inning stint in Washington last Saturday that Petit realized the roll he was on.

What Petit was chasing had never been done before, but it wasn't a daunting challenge, not for a pitcher who has overcome so much. The Giants took a flyer on Petit before the 2012 season because Jose Alguacil, an instructor in the organization, raved about the veteran right-hander's success in the Venezuelan Winter League. Petit was so lightly regarded that at the age of 27 he spent his first spring with the Giants toiling away in minor league camp. Before finally breaking through late last season, Petit cleared waivers on two separate occasions.

He has found permanence this year as a long reliever and spot starter, an invaluable Swiss army knife for manager Bruce Bochy. Petit has been dominant out of the bullpen, but it still took a month's worth of Tim Lincecum's struggles to get him back in the rotation.

In the meantime, Petit was dominating like no other pitcher in baseball. The incredible streak started

innocuously on July 22, when taking the ball in place of the injured Matt Cain, Petit gave up five runs in five innings against Philadelphia. Grady Sizemore's grounder back to the mound ended his day but started the streak.

Moved back to the bullpen after the acquisition of Jake Peavy, Petit retired six Dodgers on July 26. Two days later he set down six Pirates in order. He pitched a perfect inning in Milwaukee on Aug. 7 and another in Kansas City three days after that. When the Giants won their protest of a rained-out game in Chicago, Petit was tabbed to pick up where Ryan Vogelsong left off. He struck out five in two innings Aug. 19. Still, the streak went unnoticed. That would change four days later in Washington.

Petit entered for a shaky Lincecum and retired 13 straight. Jayson Werth, Ian Desmond and Anthony Rendon were among his five strikeout victims. It was that day that Petit and teammates started to take note of what was happening.

"It's really incredible if you think about it," Bochy said, smiling wide. "This game has been played a long time. That's quite a record."

Petit attacked it Thursday, getting three quick outs in the first to tie Jim Barr's franchise and National League record. Around him, teammates had varying degrees of knowledge about what was going on. The dugout rules are clear about how to treat a pitcher working on a perfect game, but there's no hard and fast way to handle a perfect run that lasts 38 days.

"I knew what was happening, but I didn't know exactly how far away he was," second baseman Joe Panik said. "And I certainly wasn't going to ask."

All over the field, teammates reacted differently. In the dugout, some counted down to Buehrle's mark, but in left field, Gregor Blanco pushed the streak out of his mind. Blanco's diving catch helped clinch Cain's perfect game in 2012, and on this day he provided with the bat, crushing a two-run homer to give Petit an early cushion.

The record front and center in his mind, Petit marched toward 46. Baseball has a way of adding flair to unforgettable moments, and so in the third, Petit was set to face former Fresno Grizzlies teammates Jackson Williams and Charlie Culberson. He struck out both on curveballs, reaching a previously untouched mark.

"I think it's a reward for all the work I put into pitching," Petit said through a translator. "I thank God for giving me another opportunity."

The streak that sneaked up on baseball ended in a flash. Opposing pitcher Jordan Lyles followed the record-setting strikeout with a double to left. Petit threw 191 pitches over eight appearances during the streak, retiring 42 different players in six parks. He struck out 21, got 17 outs in the air and eight on the ground.

By doing something no pitcher has ever done, Petit also did more than enough to keep a firm grip on a rotation spot. Bochy, fresh off a clubhouse champagne toast, wouldn't fully commit to Petit making another start in place of Lincecum, but there wasn't much parsing needed.

"That's a pretty good effort," he said. "We'll talk about it, but it's hard to change that with the job he did." ■

YUSMEIRO PETIT APPEARED IN 39 GAMES FOR THE GIANTS DURING THE 2014 REGULAR SEASON, INCLUDING 12 STARTS. (DAN HONDA/STAFF)

GIANTS' DIXIE HEART ON DISPLAY

BUMGARNER, PEAVY, POSEY HEAD GROUP OF SOUTHERN BOYS

BY TIM KAWAKAMI ✦ OCTOBER 19, 2014

SAN FRANCISCO—Three sons of the South have taken over a corner of the Giants clubhouse and it has only made everything twangier, tougher, funnier and better.

North Carolinian Madison Bumgarner was there first. Then came Alabamian Tim Hudson and finally Jake Peavy, another Alabamian, after he was acquired in a July trade with Boston.

And suddenly this deep corner of the Giants clubhouse — which some of them call "The Hills" — started to feel like a slice of the Deep South in the middle of the Bay Area.

So, yes, as they prepare to start the World Series in Kansas City, everything about the Giants these days is drenched with a vibrant Southern sensibility and spoken with a bit of a Southern accent.

"I like my rednecks there," manager Bruce Bochy said with a chortle during the Giants' workout Saturday.

"They're a good bunch of guys. They come out, they get after it, they play the game right."

Bochy also quickly added that the Giants roster is filled with players from all over the country and all over the world, including a vital group of Venezuelans, and that diversity is a great thing for a clubhouse.

But Bochy — who was born in France but grew up in North Carolina — also confirmed that he put in a special order with the team chef that shows where his heart and taste buds lie.

"I said listen, 'We've got some Southerners here, we need some grits,'" Bochy said. "So every day game, there's grits."

The heart of the matter: The team's best two players (Bumgarner and catcher Buster Posey) and two very vocal veterans (Hudson and Peavy) are proud Southerners.

To add to the drawl-influence, you can add Texans Hunter Pence and Brandon Belt, Floridian Michael Morse, Georgian Hunter Strickland and injured Tennessean Matt Cain.

Of course, the joke among the Southerners is that Cain — who lives in Scottsdale, Arizona, during the off-season — doesn't quite qualify, and even the stolid Posey scrunched up his face when asked if he counts Cain among the group.

That's life in the Giants clubhouse these days, and it's largely playing to a bouncy country-rock soundtrack.

"We're all country boys at heart and play a kids' game for a living that we love," said Hudson, who grew

JAKE PEAVY TALKS TO CATCHER BUSTER POSEY DURING GAME 2 OF THE WORLD SERIES. BOTH ENDS OF THE BATTERY HAIL FROM THE SOUTH — PEAVY FROM ALABAMA AND POSEY FROM GEORGIA. (NHAT V. MEYER/STAFF)

up in Phenix City, Alabama. "It's easy to get along with people you have a lot in common with."

And there's Bochy, who sets the tone and now is riding this Southern wave. But is he really a Southerner?

"Aww, yes," Peavy said with a laugh. "Skip might be from France but he's got a lot of those deep South qualities in him."

This is a team that uses the Marshall Tucker Band's "Fire on the Mountain" as an anthem because it's Bumgarner's anthem.

This is a team that wears its heart on its sleeve, that fights happily and hungrily through every out and every pitch, that has taken to the Bay Area and in return has been warmly adopted by this very metropolitan region.

"I just think that's what's great about this city," said Posey, who grew up in Leesburg, Georgia, a town of fewer than 3,000 about three hours south of Atlanta, "because it embraces all types of people. I think that's what it's known for."

In a diverse region, the Giants' diversity is significant; and it's powerful to see a group of Southerners feeling so much at home in San Francisco.

"I think I fit in great," said Peavy, born and reared in Mobile, Alabama. "I've had a blast being out and about and getting to know the city, getting to know people in the city.

"Yeah, I talk a little bit different. Other than that, I feel like we have a lot of the same things in common. It's a great place to be."

Of course, any franchise that has featured Willie Mays, Willie McCovey and Will Clark has a strong history with Southern icons.

But this team — going for its third World Series in five seasons — is especially pushed and fueled by that clubhouse corner and its Southern influence.

"I think the intensity maybe is a little bit different than it has been in the past," said shortstop Brandon Crawford, a wry East Bay native.

"Guys like Peavy and Huddy and Morse kind of their show their emotions a little bit more than guys we've had before.

"I think this group's probably a little more fiery than we've had."

Especially with Bumgarner, the pride of Hickory, N.C., taking on a larger and larger role, and with Hudson and Peavy added to the rotation, this team is looser, maybe, tougher and more expressive.

There is more laughing now, and more bite.

"It's definitely added some flavor," said Ryan Vogelsong, whose locker is on the end of the Bumgarner-Peavy row and who quickly adds that he was born in North Carolina before moving to Pennsylvania as a child.

"Basically I'm just trying to fit in and get a little redneck in me. They've got me wearing cowboy boots, so that's a start."

In fact, Peavy recently arranged for his personal boot guy to measure and design new boots for several of his younger teammates and team staffers.

Asked about the expense — easily in the tens of thousands — Peavy shrugged and said he was happy to do it.

"Just showing my appreciation to some of my coaches and my teammates," Peavy said.

You can call that hospitality or generosity or friendship, but it's all part of the Giants' Southern pull this season, and their Southern soul. ■

MADISON BUMGARNER, FROM NORTH CAROLINA, LED A POSTSEASON ROTATION THAT FEATURED THREE PROUD SOUTHERNERS — BUMGARNER AND ALABAMIANS TIM HUDSON AND JAKE PEAVY. (NHAT V. MEYER/STAFF)

BACK SURGERY ENDS PAGAN'S SEASON EARLY

BULGING BACK DISC SIDELINES OFFENSIVE CATALYST

By Alex Pavlovic ✦ September 24, 2014

LOS ANGELES—The announcement had started to seem inevitable. It was still crushing for a Giants team hoping to have another deep October run.

Center fielder Angel Pagan will have surgery on a bulging disc in his back, ending his season. The instrumental leadoff hitter is expected to be sidelined for about three months.

"It was just time to get something done," manager Bruce Bochy said. "This thing has been nagging him for three or four months. It's not getting better. We'll get it done now so he can have a full go in spring training. There was no sense in trying (to keep playing). This wasn't going to work."

Now the Giants have to figure out how to make the lineup work without a player who might be their most irreplaceable. They are 56-35 when Pagan starts and just 29-37 when he doesn't. Pagan will finish his third season in San Francisco with a .300 average, .342 on-base percentage, 21 doubles, 56 runs and 16 stolen bases.

"You have to deal with these things," Bochy said. "Injuries are unfortunately a part of the game. The important thing for us to do is what we normally do when this happens. Don't talk about it. Don't dwell on it. Keep your focus."

Renowned spinal surgeon Dr. Robert Watkins will perform the procedure — a discectomy — in Los Angeles on Thursday. Pagan said the procedure involves "sucking

THE GIANTS WERE DEALT A BLOW WHEN THEY LOST LEADOFF HITTER ANGEL PAGAN IN LATE SEPTEMBER. PAGAN FINISHED HIS SEASON WITH A .300 AVERAGE, .342 ON-BASE PERCENTAGE, 21 DOUBLES, 56 RUNS AND 16 STOLEN BASES. (DAN HONDA/STAFF)

out portions of the disc" that are causing inflammation and pain in nerves in Pagan's lower back. He said surgery was necessary to make sure there was no long-term damage.

"I have to make sure I'm 100 percent for next year," Pagan said. "It was a tough one, especially in the situation we have. I was trying. I did the best I could with the injury. But I got to a point where I couldn't function."

Pagan missed 44 games during the summer because of the same back ailment. When he returned, he was often pulled from the lineup in the late innings or a late scratch. Pagan didn't play in Phoenix last week, the first sign that something was again seriously wrong. He played in just one of the first seven games of this trip and saw Dr. Watkins on Monday. This time, the determination was that Pagan needed surgery.

Without Pagan, Bochy had Gregor Blanco in the leadoff spot Tuesday and said that's how he will handle this for the time being. Juan Perez, Chris Dominguez, Gary Brown and Travis Ishikawa are options to play left field with Blanco shifted over to center. The Giants already are playing without Matt Cain (season-ending elbow surgery) and have gone practically the entire season without Marco Scutaro (back strain).

"It kind of sucks," first baseman Brandon Belt said. "He'll be missed, but at the same time, other guys have to step up. We have the team to do it. We have the team to win. We're no strangers to this. This team has gone through this before and we know what we have to do."

Pagan, 33, has played just 167 games in the first two seasons of a four-year, $40 million deal he signed in December of 2012. When he first got hurt, the Giants were hopeful that any procedure could be pushed back to the offseason.

"I guess you always held onto hope with Angel that he would come back," Bochy said. "Now you know where you stand, so you move forward." ∎

BY UNDERGOING SURGERY ON HIS BULGING BACK DISC IN SEPTEMBER RATHER THAN WAITING UNTIL THE OFF-SEASON, ANGEL PAGAN HOPED TO BE A FULL PARTICIPANT IN SPRING TRAINING IN 2015. (DAN HONDA/STAFF)

GIANTS CLINCH PLAYOFF BERTH

BREWERS' DEFEAT SENDS S.F. TO POSTSEASON

BY ALEX PAVLOVIC ✦ SEPTEMBER 26, 2014

SAN FRANCISCO—Hunter Pence was packing up and getting ready to head for the ballpark when he heard the news. Brandon Crawford didn't know until he got a congratulatory text from a relative. Tim Hudson first heard when his excited wife called as he drove to the ballpark.

Few of the Giants players were actually watching the Milwaukee Brewers and Cincinnati Reds on Thursday afternoon, but Bruce Bochy was avidly tuned into the MLB app on his iPad as the Reds won, clinching a wild-card playoff spot for Bochy and the Giants.

"We would have loved to come crashing in the front door instead of the back door," Bochy said. "But this works."

All along, the Giants had planned to celebrate their inclusion in the postseason, but they were hoping it wouldn't be an awkward affair that came after a loss. A three-run rally in the eighth inning against the San Diego Padres guaranteed a 9-8 win and good vibes all the way around.

"I couldn't be prouder of these guys. ... It's been a tough year," Bochy said during the postgame celebration.

About 15 hours after the Giants watched the Dodgers clinch the division, the Reds beat the Brewers 5-3, officially setting the field in the National League. If the current standings hold, the Giants will travel to Pittsburgh for a winner-advances matchup.

"We've got a shot to win one game and move on," Buster Posey said.

While Bochy wouldn't make an official announcement Thursday, Madison Bumgarner is on track to start that game. Bochy smiled and said reporters could easily speculate about the decision he will make, later adding that Bumgarner wouldn't pitch Sunday and the Giants were looking at other options for the last game of the regular season, including right-hander Tim Lincecum.

Bumgarner will finish the season with an 18-10 record, 2.98 ERA and a career-high 219 strikeouts in 217⅓ innings. He pitched into the eighth in his last start and hit a two-run homer, giving the Giants a highlight to hold onto during a stretch that has been rough on a banged-up roster. Bochy hoped the news that the Giants were officially in the postseason would take some pressure off.

"They've had a tough week," he said. "Something like this can lift their spirits."

The bats finally took off on a day when players

GIANTS OUTFIELDER HUNTER PENCE CELEBRATES IN THE VICTORIOUS LOCKER ROOM AFTER SAN FRANCISCO'S WIN OVER THE SAN DIEGO PADRES SENT THE GIANTS TO THE NATIONAL LEAGUE WILD-CARD GAME — ITS THIRD PLAYOFF BERTH IN FIVE SEASONS. (AP IMAGES)

the better. It's a tremendous accomplishment of everybody in here to make the playoffs."

The early clinch could lead to some lineup changes down the stretch. Bochy talked to Posey, Sandoval and Pence about taking some time off over the final three games to make sure the key bats are fresh for October.

The decision to push Bumgarner back shows the Giants care more about having their ace lined up for the season's most important game than about where it's played, but the Giants still have some business to take care of. With Michael Morse unlikely to play anytime soon, Bochy tried Travis Ishikawa out in left field, hoping to find a semi-permanent solution to a hole created when Angel Pagan had back surgery on September 25.

"I'll see how he looks," Bochy said. "He's a pretty good athlete."

Ishikawa looked fine in his first career start in the outfield, but the Giants didn't look comfortable with a big lead. Homers by Brandon Belt and Crawford helped the Giants jump out to a 6-0 advantage, but the bullpen gave it back in a span of two innings.

Will Venable and Yasmani Grandal went deep in the sixth, ending Yusmeiro Petit's day. Javier Lopez and Jean Machi got into a mess in the seventh, and Machi gave up a go-ahead grand slam to Grandal as Lincecum and Sergio Romo raced for the bullpen mound. Before Bochy could insert Lincecum, Machi gave up a solo shot to Rene Rivera that put the Padres up 8-6.

The Giants stormed right back. Pablo Sandoval's fourth RBI came on a seventh-inning single that cut the deficit to one. The Giants had four singles in the inning, including one from Belt that tied the game. Pence scored the go-ahead run moments later when Matt Duffy laid down a perfect safety squeeze bunt.

Romo and Santiago Casilla held the lead, guaranteeing that the Giants could celebrate a win and a postseason berth at the same time. ■

started preparing for the champagne-and-beer-soaked celebration as they arrived at the park. As Pablo Sandoval sat at his locker and looked at his phone, scuba goggles rested on his chest. Pence bounced around as he talked about the importance of celebrating the achievement. The right fielder pushed for a celebration of the wild-card clinch, brushing off any thoughts that it was beneath a clubhouse that is full of World Series champions.

"It's the carrot in front of the horse," he said. "In spring training and the offseason you put that seed in there, like, 'We're pouring champagne on each other.' That's the draw. That's why it's there. I think the more you can enjoy accomplishments and make the best of it,

CASILLA EMBRACES ROLE

VETERAN'S TEAM-FIRST STYLE EASES GIANTS' MIDSEASON TRANSITION AT CLOSER

By Carl Steward + October 10, 2014

SAN FRANCISCO—Santiago Casilla seemed frazzled as he faced the dangerous Bryce Harper to close out the N.L. Division Series. After getting two quick strikes, Casilla's pitches suddenly started flying all over the place, and he appeared to have lost his rhythm and nerve for the situation.

But Casilla knew exactly what he was doing. Having watched Harper's towering home run off rookie Hunter Strickland a few innings before, Casilla simply wasn't going to give the young Washington Nationals slugger anything he could drive out of the park, especially after he nearly squared up one of his fastballs and fouled it off.

"I say, 'Go to first base, it's better, hang out over there,'" Casilla said of Harper, reframing the moment with a wide smile. "You want to swing, swing in the dirt."

With the less threatening, right-handed hitting Wilson Ramos on deck, Casilla, who limited righty batters to a .161 average this year, knew it was the logical move. Ramos grounded out weakly to second base, and the Giants were on to St. Louis for the N.L. Championship Series.

Earlier in his career, Casilla might have challenged Harper. But at age 34 and now in his 11th season, wisdom has become an integral part of his repertoire to go along with his devastating sinking fastball, curve and slider.

"I'm smarter this year," he said. "I think more about location with my pitching now. A couple of years ago, I made a lot of mistakes. Now I try to take it easy on the mound and just be in focus on my pitches."

It shows. Even with a late May hamstring injury that kept him out for nearly a month, Casilla had his best year, whether he was setting up or closing. He posted a 1.70 ERA, a career low. Walking just 15 hitters in 54 appearances covering 58⅓ innings, he posted an 0.86 WHIP, also an all-time low. He allowed just three home runs all year, all in one-sided Giants wins. After assuming the closer role from Sergio Romo in early July, he saved 19 games and blew just one, and the Giants wound up winning that game.

But perhaps the most significant development is how Casilla and Romo exchanged roles so seamlessly — and agreeably — and seemed to benefit from the switch.

SANTIAGO CASILLA POSTED A 1.70 ERA IN THE 2014 SEASON, A CAREER LOW. HE TOOK OVER THE CLOSER ROLE FROM SERGIO ROMO MIDSEASON. (JOSIE LEPE/STAFF)

Returning to his eighth-inning role, Romo didn't give up a run in 11 August appearances and has given up just two runs since July 22. Casilla, meanwhile, has given up just one run since Sept. 1. The only walk he's allowed since August was his semi-intentional pass to Harper on Tuesday night.

Manager Bruce Bochy said that as well as Casilla has pitched, much credit goes to Romo.

"What a great job he's done setting aside his own ego and agenda and accepting the eighth-inning role," Bochy said. "He was the closer here, and it's not easy sometimes. But he never said anything, never complained, and for a manager, you appreciate that. That's the only way this works."

Casilla might have helped, too. When Bochy made the switch, the pitcher went to Romo and told him he wasn't trying to take his job. He told him he didn't consider himself the closer.

"I told him, 'Don't feel bad,'" Casilla said. "I'm just here to do my job. It doesn't matter what innings. I still don't feel like I'm the closer. I work for the Giants. I'm just happy to win, you know?"

To wit, Casilla started the 2012 season as the closer, but when he hit rough patch in July, he was supplanted by Romo and the Giants went on to win the World Series with both pitchers acting as major contributors. So this isn't a new storyline. It's just that the roles are reversed.

"I think either one of them can close, and the other one can pitch the eighth," catcher Buster Posey said. "One of the reasons we've had success the past few years is guys are able to set their egos aside and perform in different roles to help the team win. Those two are a really great example of that."

It helps, too, that Casilla doesn't embellish his new role with theatrics. He doesn't shoot imaginary arrows into the air after finishing a game. He doesn't thump his chest. He doesn't have heavy metal warm-up music. Outfielder Gregor Blanco noted that the most demonstrative thing the deeply religious Casilla might do is kneel and pray after a good game, and he'll do that quietly in the dugout.

Posey thinks Casilla's selfless, unflashy demeanor is the primary reason he's overlooked as one of the best in the game at what he does.

"He doesn't have that cool, signature move," he said. "He just goes about his business and gets the job done. But he's got electric stuff. That's the main thing. He's able to get guys out sometimes even when they know what's coming. And like a lot of guys on our staff, he's just a really great competitor." ■

OPPOSITE: SANTIAGO CASILLA EARNED HIS SECOND SAVE OF THE NATIONAL LEAGUE CHAMPIONSHIP SERIES AGAINST THE ST. LOUIS CARDINALS IN GAME 4. (DOUG DURAN/STAFF) ABOVE: CASILLA AND CATCHER BUSTER POSEY CELEBRATE AFTER CLOSING OUT THE GIANTS IN GAME 4 OF THE NLCS. (JANE TYSKA/STAFF)

40

PITCHER

MADISON BUMGARNER

PITCHER'S USUALLY CALM DEMEANOR BELIES HIS INTENSITY ON MOUND

BY ALEX PAVLOVIC ✦ OCTOBER 11, 2014

ST. LOUIS—You walk the Giants clubhouse with the same question in mind, and often you get the same answer. Tell us about the fire that burns inside Madison Bumgarner.

"You've seen the YouTube video, right?" his teammates respond.

We have, and four years and two rings later, it's still instructive. Bumgarner, the then-20-year-old ready to take on the world — and soon the World Series — was ejected from a Triple-A game in June 2010 after a series of questionable calls. He was restrained by teammates and pulled off the field, exchanging words with Sacramento River Cats instructor Rickey Henderson on his way to the dugout, according to eyewitnesses. One former Fresno Grizzlies staffer swears there was a frantic search for Bumgarner's truck keys out of fear he was going to drive onto the field.

The outburst led to a three-game suspension and fine from the Pacific Coast League, and the Giants tacked on a fine, as well. But they weren't exactly upset with their prospect. The video made the rounds, with most focusing on Bumgarner — on his way off the field — angrily throwing the baseball deep into the outfield.

"We thought that was a lot of arm strength," Giants vice president of player personnel Dick Tidrow said recently, smiling.

Bruce Bochy, then in his fourth year with the Giants, watched the clip before Bumgarner was called up later that month. He wanted to know what the Giants had on their hands, and he loved what he saw. His pitching coach, Dave Righetti, had made a similar throw as a Yankee.

"You saw it right there," Bochy said. "You saw the fire."

In 2014, the baseball world has seen it.

Bumgarner is the Giants' ace and a burgeoning leader in the clubhouse at age 25. He leads by example, and often it's an explosive one. Bumgarner is the Giants pitcher most likely to throw at an opponent he deems to have crossed a line.

Twice this year, he clashed with Dodgers star Yasiel Puig. It was not lost on the Giants clubhouse that Puig slowly backed off when Bumgarner threw his glove down during a confrontation at Dodger Stadium in September. These are the moments when Bumgarner lets the fire out, despite his best efforts.

"I don't like anybody to be able to tell how I'm

GIANTS ACE MADISON BUMGARNER SET A MAJOR LEAGUE POSTSEASON RECORD WITH 26 $^2/_3$ CONSECUTIVE SCORELESS INNINGS ON THE ROAD IN GAME 1 OF THE NATIONAL LEAGUE CHAMPIONSHIP SERIES. (NHAT V. MEYER/STAFF)

try to generate it into concentration and focus. He's that way, too, but you can see he lets it out every once in a while. He's a gamer."

That quality was already shining through when the Giants picked Bumgarner 10th overall out of North Carolina's South Caldwell High in 2007. Tidrow couldn't take his eyes off the tall, well-built kid with an easy crossfire delivery. He was sold because of one trait.

"He was one of the few high school pitchers I had ever seen pitch inside," Tidrow said. "I thought at the time that he wasn't afraid of much, and I don't think that's changed. He's always been fearless. It's how he was brought up. It's in his DNA. It's hard for a guy with his release point to pitch inside to right-handed hitters, but he just repeated it and repeated it. I had never seen that before."

Bumgarner still does it that way, moving his fastball across planes and sections of the plate to set up hitters. The style is hell on opponents, because Bumgarner, his arm sweeping well behind his body and then back toward the plate, would be deceptive even if he weren't a master at hitting his spots.

"He's one of the more unorthodox pitchers you're ever going to face," Cardinals star Matt Carpenter said. "There aren't a whole lot of guys like him in terms of arm angles and where he's coming after you."

Tidrow saw another trait on those afternoons in North Carolina that made Bumgarner an easy pick for the Giants. This one showed at the plate.

"He always took big swings, and that showed me a guy that wasn't afraid," Tidrow said. "He was not afraid to look bad."

Bumgarner rarely does, and he does his best to look calm, too. But sometimes, like that night in Fresno, the inner fire is on full display.

"I like to just try to keep the same demeanor no matter what's happening," he said. "It's obviously easier said than done sometimes." ■

feeling," he said. "I try to stay even keel, and I don't want you guys, or the other team, or the fans or anyone to know where my head is at, even though sometimes it's probably in some bad places."

It's rare that Bumgarner actually breaks from character, but he does send a not-so-subtle hint about what's underneath that beard and calm stare as he takes the mound. Bumgarner's warm-up song is "Fire on the Mountain" by the Marshall Tucker Band, and teammates say the intensity is there even when it's not showing, as it does so clearly with famously fiery righthanders Jake Peavy and Ryan Vogelsong.

"He's up there. He's probably just as intense as both of us, but we all do it in our different ways," Vogelsong said. "Jake is pretty vocal, and I kind of hold it in and

ABOVE: MADISON BUMGARNER DELIVERS THE FINAL PITCH OF HIS SHUTOUT PERFORMANCE IN GAME 5 OF THE 2014 WORLD SERIES. (DOUG DURAN/STAFF) OPPOSITE: BUMGARNER'S DOMINANT PERFORMANCE IN GAME 1 OF THE NLCS INCLUDED GIVING UP JUST FOUR HITS IN 7²/₃ INNINGS. (NHAT V. MEYER/STAFF)

28

CATCHER

BUSTER POSEY

CATCHER PUTS ON CLINIC BEHIND HOME PLATE

By Mark Purdy ♦ October 11, 2014

ST. LOUIS—Can't tell you which team will win this Giants-Cardinals series. Can tell you which position on the field will likely decide the winner.

Hint: Players at that position wear masks.

Buster Posey is the Giants' two-time World Series winning catcher who has won a National League MVP award. Yadier Molina is the Cardinals' two-time World Series winning catcher who has won six gold gloves. Both men will be in the center of everything when the series begins.

Can't tell you which catcher will perform better over the next four to seven games. Can tell you which catcher I'd want behind the plate, calling pitches.

With apologies to Molina, who is unquestionably a top tier defensive catcher in terms of receiving and throwing, I would choose Posey.

Molina might scoop and hurl better. But watching Posey over the past 10 days of this postseason — and really, for the past five years — it continually strikes me how underrated he is in the category of calling the correct pitches at the correct times from whichever man is on the mound for the Giants.

Andrew Susac, who backs up Posey, occasionally feels as if he is attending catching graduate school when he sees Posey at work.

"I'll be sitting on the bench, watching him," Susac said. "And he'll call a pitch and I'll go: 'Really? Oh yeah, I see what he's doing. That's smart.'" Results do not lie: The Washington Nationals batted .253 as a team during the 2014 regular season. They batted .164 in their series loss to the Giants. Jayson Werth, a .292 hitter, went 1 for 17 over the four games. Denard Span, a .302 hitter, went 2 for 19.

The Giants pitching staff executed all of those deliveries to get all of those outs. But it was Posey who called those pitches.

Can't tell you what Posey thinks is his best quality as a catcher because he'll never give that up. Can tell you that, if pinned down, he will acknowledge that calling those pitches is something he enjoys as much or

BUSTER POSEY ROUNDS SECOND BASE ON PABLO SANDOVAL'S FIRST-INNING DOUBLE IN GAME 1 OF THE WORLD SERIES. THE 2010 NL ROOKIE OF THE YEAR AND 2012 MVP BATTED .311 WITH 22 HOME RUNS AND 89 RBIs IN 2014. (D. ROSS CAMERON/STAFF)

more than anything about the job.

But the interesting part is how he goes about that job.

Posey, often reluctant to talk about his method, does own up to having his own way of doing things when it comes to following the book on certain batters. "I spend time doing that," Posey said of studying data on opposing hitters, "but it's not a huge amount of time. You want to know a batter's weaknesses and strengths, but I don't like to be tied down to it. You've got to adjust with the game."

The human element at work! Imagine that, in this day and age. Like every major league team before a series, the Giants leave a printout of the entire scouting report at every player's locker stall, including Posey's. There is also a players-only website that Posey can consult to call up granular stats on every opposing batter — which pitches they swing at and miss the most, which ones they take the most, and so forth. He can also call up video of every opponent's at-bat against a Giants pitcher or any other pitcher. Posey consults all of that information. But then he'll go out on the field and selectively ignore it. He will instead react instinctively to what he's seeing in the moment — from his own pitcher, from opposing batters, from how the umpire is calling the strike zone, perhaps even how the wind is blowing and which balls are carrying to which fields.

BUSTER POSEY TALKS TO RELIEVER HUNTER STRICKLAND DURING THE NINTH INNING OF GAME 1 OF THE WORLD SERIES. POSEY'S GAME-CALLING HAS ANCHORED A GIANTS PITCHING STAFF THAT HAS WON THREE WORLD SERIES IN POSEY'S FIVE MAJOR LEAGUE SEASONS. (JOSIE LEPE/STAFF)

"He's got a game plan," Susac said. "He gets the report. But I don't even think he reads it through that much. He'll look at the computer for a while, but he gets out there and goes with the flow and with the rhythm of the game. To be honest, I think he's naturally gifted in calling a game. I learn a lot by watching him. You know, sometimes the scouting report will say a batter should get curveballs down and away in the zone — even though you just got him out on fastballs. So do you stick with the report? Or go with what you're seeing in front of you?"

Can't tell you how much longer Posey will play catcher. Can tell you why the Giants are so reluctant to move him away from the position.

It's because of all the stuff discussed above, and more.

When people talk about Posey moving to first base or third base sooner or later — and the fan sentiment seems to be on the side of sooner because of the wear-and-tear of catching — they are thinking mostly of keeping Posey's bat in the lineup. There's not much thought given to how much the Giants would lose from someone else handling the team's pitchers, how many runs it might cost the Giants per game. Is it an accident that the only World Series titles won by the team in San Francisco have been with Posey behind the plate? It is not.

Coincidentally, both managers in this series — Mike Matheny of the Cardinals and Bruce Bochy of the Giants — were catchers during their major league careers. And each of the former catchers obviously loves his own current catcher. So asking for comparisons would be folly. However, I asked Matheny and Bochy to rank the most important parts of a catcher's defensive tool kit in terms of qualities most necessary to win. Their replies were remarkably similar.

Matheny's answer: "It's consciousness. A catcher who wants to be in the middle of everything and has an eye and a mind that's ready for every pitch and every scenario and looking for an edge, an advantage, wherever it can be found. That kind of leads itself into leadership, which I would put right below. Then all the tangibles."

Bochy's answer: "You start with how they handle the pitcher. How they handle the staff. The game-calling part, that's what you look at. And of course, the receiving then, handling pitches … That should be his priority, handling the staff."

You could use all those words to describe the strength of Posey — and Molina, as well. Keep an eye on them both over the next week or so. But especially keep an eye on Posey as he works with Madison Bumgarner in Game 1, followed by the Giants pitchers in every game thereafter. Watch the Posey machinery at work.

Listening to Matheny and Bochy, I was thinking back to the series clincher by the Giants over Washington. I was thinking about how, in the ninth inning with two outs and the Giants ahead by just one run, Posey made certain that reliever Santiago Casilla did not give Nationals slugger Bryce Harper anything to hit that might tie the game. Instead, Harper wound up getting a base on balls. Posey then called for a Casilla pitch that induced the next Washington batter, Wilson Ramos, to ground out and win the game. Smart stuff.

Can't tell you where the Giants would be without Posey calling those pitches. Can tell you they don't want to find out. ■

12

INFIELDER

JOE PANIK

INFIELDER SUCCEEDS ON BIG STAGE BY PLAYING IT COOL

BY MARCUS THOMPSON II ✦ OCTOBER 19, 2014

SAN FRANCISCO—Joe Panik knows he's not normal.

The way he bullies his nerves. The way he rebuffs pressure. The way he tunes out doubt and failure. It's an uncanny ability, especially for a 23-year-old rookie who was in Triple-A not even four months ago.

Panik struggles to explain it outside of his parents being the same way. But it's the reason he has emerged as a pivotal player for the Giants on this World Series run.

Second base was once a weakness for the Giants. Now it's rock solid.

That's a testament to Panik's composure.

"You don't see that from many rookies," shortstop Brandon Crawford said. "It took him a couple weeks to adjust to the big league level. After that, he's been a really consistent No. 2 hitter and second baseman. These situations aren't too big for him."

Brittany Pinto worried that they might be. Wanting to offer emotional support, Panik's longtime girlfriend tried to break through his cool exterior.

She tried to imagine the enormity of having to prove yourself as a rookie — on a good team, no less. She tried to fathom how the sting of bad games and missed opportunities might linger. Or how success sometimes swells the ego.

Though she has known Panik since they were kids, she still marvels at the poise he has shown since being inserted into the Giants lineup in June.

When he committed two errors in his fourth game, or while he was mustering just 15 hits in his first 70 at-bats (a .214 average), or when he got hot with the bat in August — no change. Same young Joe.

"Every morning, I'd ask him how he was doing," said Pinto, who went to high school with Panik in Hopewell Junction, New York. "He just says 'I'm good.' No nerves. No nothing. And I'm like 'How do you stay so calm like that?' I'm usually freaking out."

Pinto should know by now. Back when Panik played Little League ball in upstate New York and people were fawning over his talent, he paid it no mind. He did show a little excitement when his high school jersey was retired. But even when his dream came true, his emotions didn't spill over.

Back in June, shortly after 2 a.m. on the East Coast, he woke his parents to tell them he was going to the big leagues. "Anybody would think he'd be jumping up and down, but he was very low-key," Panik's father, Paul, told the *Poughkeepsie (N.Y.) Journal*. "He called us and

ROOKIE SECOND BASEMAN JOE PANIK BURST ONTO THE POSTSEASON SCENE FOR THE GIANTS IN THE NATIONAL LEAGUE DIVISION SERIES AGAINST THE WASHINGTON NATIONALS. HE SCORED THREE RUNS IN THE FOUR-GAME SERIES. (NHAT V. MEYER/STAFF)

in the clubhouse. He has seen the rookie go through ups and downs. Blanco said on bad days and good, Panik put in the same amount of work, kept his approach consistent.

"He handled himself well," Blanco said. "When he first got here, nobody believed in him. Everybody was saying we should go out and get whoever. He wanted to show he belongs and he did.

"I'm so proud of him. I really see what he's accomplished. The way he prepares every game. He loves the game. He's really quiet, but he is passionate about it."

Finally, Panik confesses to a time he wasn't so chill.

"There was one time, I'll tell you," Panik says. "The day I got drafted."

said, 'This is it.' I think he was stunned. It was just matter of fact, just kind of the way he is."

Panik said he gets that even keel from his parents. Because of the trait he inherited, Panik has been able to let his talent shine on the biggest stage of his life.

It prevents him from pressing at the plate, which is how he batted .379 in August, how he got five hits in his first two playoff games, how he broke the Giants' home run drought with a two-run bomb in Game 5 of the NLCS to get the home team back in it.

"You can't let the moment get too big," Panik said. "Stay calm and cool, focus on what you've got to take care of. You've got to block out everything else around you so you can do what you do best."

It's not that Panik doesn't feel the emotions. He does get frustrated and excited. He does get nervous.

Center fielder Gregor Blanco lockers next to Panik

Panik said the wall came down that day in 2011, when he learned the Giants took him in the first round with the 29th overall pick. He doesn't feel comfortable talking about it. He doesn't admit he cried or describe how he "showed some emotion and let it out."

Maybe going there would have forced him to realize the moment after Game 5 in which he was engulfed: celebratory suds flying, teammates hugging, "Wake Me Up" by Avicci blasting in the background, an NLCS championship cap on his head, his girlfriend by his side. Maybe if he turns off his special skill, he might lose it again.

Joe Chill can't let that happen.

"I can't thank my parents enough for giving me that trait," he says. "I see a lot of people just letting emotions fly and sometimes it gets the best of them. That's why I stay cool." ∎

ABOVE: IN HIS FIRST NATIONAL LEAGUE DIVISION SERIES GAME OF HIS CAREER, JOE PANIK LED THE GIANTS TO A WIN OVER THE NATIONALS WITH TWO HITS AND AN RBI AS WELL AS A CRUCIAL STOP IN THE SEVENTH. (NHAT V. MEYER/ STAFF) OPPOSITE: SAN FRANCISCO GIANTS SECOND BASEMAN JOE PANIK TAKES THE THROW FROM BUSTER POSEY IN TIME TO CATCH KANSAS CITY'S ALCIDES ESCOBAR ATTEMPTING TO STEAL SECOND BASE IN THE FIRST INNING OF GAME 2 OF THE WORLD SERIES. (D. ROSS CAMERON/STAFF)

OUTFIELDER

HUNTER PENCE

OUTFIELDER PLAYS WITH A STYLE THAT'S ALL HIS OWN

By Alex Pavlovic ✦ July 14, 2014

SAN FRANCISCO—Young Hunter Pence was heartbroken.

The energetic Little Leaguer coveted the number seven that his older brother wore, but it was taken. So Howard Pence came up with a solution, telling his son that eight was a good fit because it was the same right side up and upside down. He explained to Hunter, a Texas power tumbling champion, that the new number would rotate with him as he did back flips.

"After that," the Giants right fielder said, "I owned eight."

When the game's biggest names line up for the All-Star game in Minneapolis, the symmetrical number will be on the back of one of the most asymmetrical stars the game has ever seen.

The rest of Pence's first-half numbers fit right in: a .297 average, 12 homers, 2.9 WAR and 67 runs, tied for second in the league. It's how Pence compiles those numbers that makes him unique.

How is he second in the league with seven outfield assists when he has a stilted, sidearm throwing motion that starts at the hip? How is one of the most upright,

frantic base runners in the majors also one of the best? How has the violent swing that seemingly changes pitch to pitch led to a .286 career average and six consecutive 20-homer seasons?

Most important, how did coaches from Little League to the majors allow Pence to keep playing this way?

"I mean, how can you change me?" Pence said. "I don't know how to do it normal, you know? The way I'm doing it is normal to me."

That's what makes Pence so fascinating to teammates, opponents and coaches who spend every free second trying to find perfection in a game where even the best hitters fail seven out of 10 times.

"Everything he does is not what you would teach anybody, anywhere," third base coach Tim Flannery said. "But somehow it all works for him."

The Giants acquired Pence from Philadelphia at the 2012 trade deadline, four days after they had picked up Marco Scutaro. The duo helped the Giants win a second World Series in three years, with Pence serving as the rousing reverend when the team fell behind in the

OUTFIELDER HUNTER PENCE HAS EMERGED AS A LEADER BOTH ON AND OFF THE FIELD FOR SAN FRANCISCO. HIS INSPIRATIONAL SPEECHES SPURRED THE GIANTS TO THEIR WORLD SERIES WIN IN 2012 AND HE DELIVERED AGAIN IN 2014. (NHAT V. MEYER/STAFF)

NLDS and Scutaro winning MVP honors a round later.

When the second baseman returned to Venezuela that offseason, the most pressing question was rarely about his first title and a .500 batting average in the league championship series.

"Everyone was asking about Hunter," Scutaro said. "They were asking, 'How crazy is he?'"

The wackiness starts before the first pitch at AT&T Park. Pence jogs to right field every night, waves to the fans in the arcade and claps his glove. Then he turns to his center fielder, sometimes Angel Pagan, sometimes Gregor Blanco. Their throws are textbook. Then there's Pence, hurtling his arm forward in a manner that looks painful.

As with other things Pence does on the field, there's a physiological reason for this. He said a physical taken before he signed a five-year, $90 million extension last September revealed that his thoracic spine (upper back) flexibility was naturally "off-the-charts horrible." Then, when Pence was 12, he hurt his shoulder and found it painful to throw over the top.

Pence adapted. He has 71 outfield assists in eight seasons, finishing in the top five in the league every year from 2008 to 2012. He led the league with 16 assists in 2008 and 2009.

Flannery says that at 31, Pence doesn't have quite as strong a throwing arm as when he was in Houston and Philadelphia, but it remains powerful and accurate. There's something else, too.

"He takes it personally when someone tries to run on him," Flannery said.

In that way, Pence's throws, while coming from an odd slot, are really originating from a deeper place.

"The main thing about Hunter is his mindset," strength coach Carl Kochan said. "He believes he will win. He believes he will make every throw and win every at-bat. He believes he will go up there and hit the ball hard. Everything is with the foot on the gas pedal."

That's why manager Bruce Bochy has taken to calling his right fielder Full Throttle. When Bochy originally saw Pence on a field, though, he had a much different thought.

"The first time I saw him, back when he was with Houston, I said, 'You're kidding me,'" Bochy recalled, laughing at the memory. "I thought it was a joke."

Bochy was stunned when he saw a warm-up swing that looks better suited for a sand trap. Even Pence had a hard time believing his eyes when the scoreboard in a visiting park focused on him one day, showing the at-the-knees swing that abruptly gets cut off.

"It was disturbing," Pence says of that first look.

While most hitters use the on-deck circle to lock in with their mechanics, Pence just stays loose, a tactic that's right in line with the way he approaches hitting. Early in his big league career, Pence found that obsessing over mechanics only messed him up, so he simplified things.

He keeps his knees bent and his upper body relaxed, making sure he's ready to be short to the ball and long through it. When he comes forward, Pence swings as hard as he possibly can, every time. That's how he's always done it, and it's here that he relies on hand-eye coordination that's sharpened with training methods more commonly found in a frat house.

Pence is a dedicated ping pong player in the offseason because it works his "fast-twitch muscles" and reaction time. He is an avid video game player during the season, and believes that games like "Mortal Kombat" help his timing and focus.

When it all comes together, Pence hits the ball as hard and as far as anybody. But even when he's off, Pence can find production.

Rarely has his inimitable swing been more apparent than on a solo homer he hit at Coors Field on May 22. Down 0-2 to right-hander Tommy Kahnle, Pence settled into his wide stance, his hands choked up on the bat to emulate the Barry Bonds poster he had as a child. He slowly tapped the front foot twice, then quickly twice more. His hands twitched as his eyes bore into Kahnle. The pitch was an elevated slider, a sure ball that had catcher Wilin Rosario reaching his glove up and toward Pence, who had opened up far too soon. The ball never got to Rosario.

His whole body now facing Kahnle, Pence somehow got the barrel around in time and lined a solo homer to right. A stunned Duane Kuiper called it an emergency swing on the broadcast.

"It's kind of embarrassing. You look at the swing and you're like, 'What the heck was that,' but when I was in there hitting, I just saw the ball," Pence said. "I know what it felt like. It caught the sweet spot of the barrel, but you look at what my body did and it just looks awful."

In an era where Little Leaguers have swing coaches and major leaguers obsess over clips on their iPads, Pence is a throwback.

"Other guys are a little bit more under control, shall we say, but it works for him," former Giants star Will Clark said. "You're going to get 100 percent max effort. It might not look good, but you're hoping you get good results."

Clark gets a ballot every season for MLB's Heart and Hustle award. Every year he writes in Pence's name, and never is the reason more clear than when Pence makes contact with the ball.

"We're going to have a lot of movement," Pence tells a group of kids. "Like a hungry man chasing a taco."

The scene was part of a spoof video Pence made with *Sports Illustrated* last season, promoting the fictional "Hunter's Hitters Youth Baseball Camp." In another clip, Pence shows the group his short-armed running form as the narrator explains that this training method is known as "running during an earthquake."

Again, this part of the game may not look fluid, but it's one Pence has mastered. The max effort combined with natural speed has turned Pence into one of the game's best runners. FanGraphs.com uses a stat called Ultimate Base Running (UBR) to account for the value a player adds on the bases. Pence leads the majors at 5.6, well ahead of runner-up Brian Dozier (4.1) of the Twins. Pence has 14 infield singles this season and is 8 for 10 in stolen base attempts.

"He might be the best base runner I've had because he's the same all the time," Flannery said. "He doesn't run any different if you're down 4-0 in the ninth or it's 4-4. He's got great instincts, he cuts the corners well,

and he scores from first better than anybody because he's in great shape and he doesn't assume you're going to stop him.

"He told me once, 'I'm a big train. Once I get going, don't stop me late.'"

Pence has given the same "don't stop me" directive to Bochy. The man who says of his job description, "I play baseball, that's awesome," has appeared in a major league best 317 consecutive games. Pence has played 855 of 860 Giants innings this year, all set to Full Throttle.

It's for that reason that his coaches implore you to look past the irregular swing, throws and running style. Look past the fiery eyes, the tongue that hangs like Jordan's on tough catches and the socks Pence pulls above his kneecaps because that's simply how he's most comfortable.

Ignore all that and watch the effort and the energy. Watch the incredible passion for a game Pence plays better than most, even as he plays it differently from all.

"It's just the way I am," Pence said. "I love it. I enjoy it. I want to just thank whatever it is that created me." ∎

HUNTER PENCE SCORED 106 RUNS IN THE 2014 REGULAR SEASON, BY FAR THE MOST OF HIS MAJOR LEAGUE CAREER. (NHAT V. MEYER/STAFF)

48

INFIELDER

PABLO SANDOVAL

LATEST STELLAR POSTSEASON FOR GIANTS' MR. OCTOBER
COULD PAY OFF BIG THIS WINTER

By Alex Pavlovic ✦ October 20, 2014

KANSAS CITY—In the tightest moments, the ones that draw the air out of a stadium, the fun-loving Panda emerges to let you exhale.

It happened in Game 5 of the N.L. Championship Series, when Pablo Sandoval dived for a ground ball, just barely tipping it to shortstop Brandon Crawford, who whirled and threw to second for an out that completed a play that kept the go-ahead run from scoring. Sandoval stepped up in Game 3, too, robbing Matt Holliday of extra bases and the go-ahead RBI.

In those moments, and there have been many of them this October, Sandoval pumps his fist and roars. He soaks in the adulation of a crowd that has seen him go through so much as a Giant, ups and downs that were largely his own doing. He has been scolded about his weight and benched in the late innings, but in his seventh year with the Giants, Sandoval wants nothing more than to be there in the big spots, exalting a team and fan base and forgetting about everything swirling around him.

He'll be a free agent at the end of the season, and this could be his final month as a Giant. This postseason will help shape his market, but Sandoval doesn't view it that way.

"Do I feel pressure? Pressure for what?" he says, laughing and throwing his hands in the air. "This is my third one, man. I'm not going to feel pressure. I'm the kind of guy that loves to play with pressure. I try to show my teammates, 'Hey, guys, we can do it in this situation. We can win every time.'"

Thanks in large part to Sandoval, the Giants are doing that. They're back in the World Series, with Sandoval's tantalizing talent once again shining bright on the October stage.

It was this time two years ago that he threw an early knockout blow at the powerful Detroit Tigers with a three-homer masterpiece that had Justin Verlander flummoxed, the Giants emboldened and earned Sandoval the World Series MVP trophy.

That night was his most brilliant as a professional and likely always will be, but it's only one chunk of Sandoval's stellar October résumé. He has reached base safely in 23

IN GAME 1 OF THE WORLD SERIES, PABLO SANDOVAL IMPROVED HIS LIFETIME POSTSEASON BATTING AVERAGE TO .328, PUTTING HIM AHEAD OF BABE RUTH IN THAT CATEGORY. (NHAT V. MEYER/STAFF)

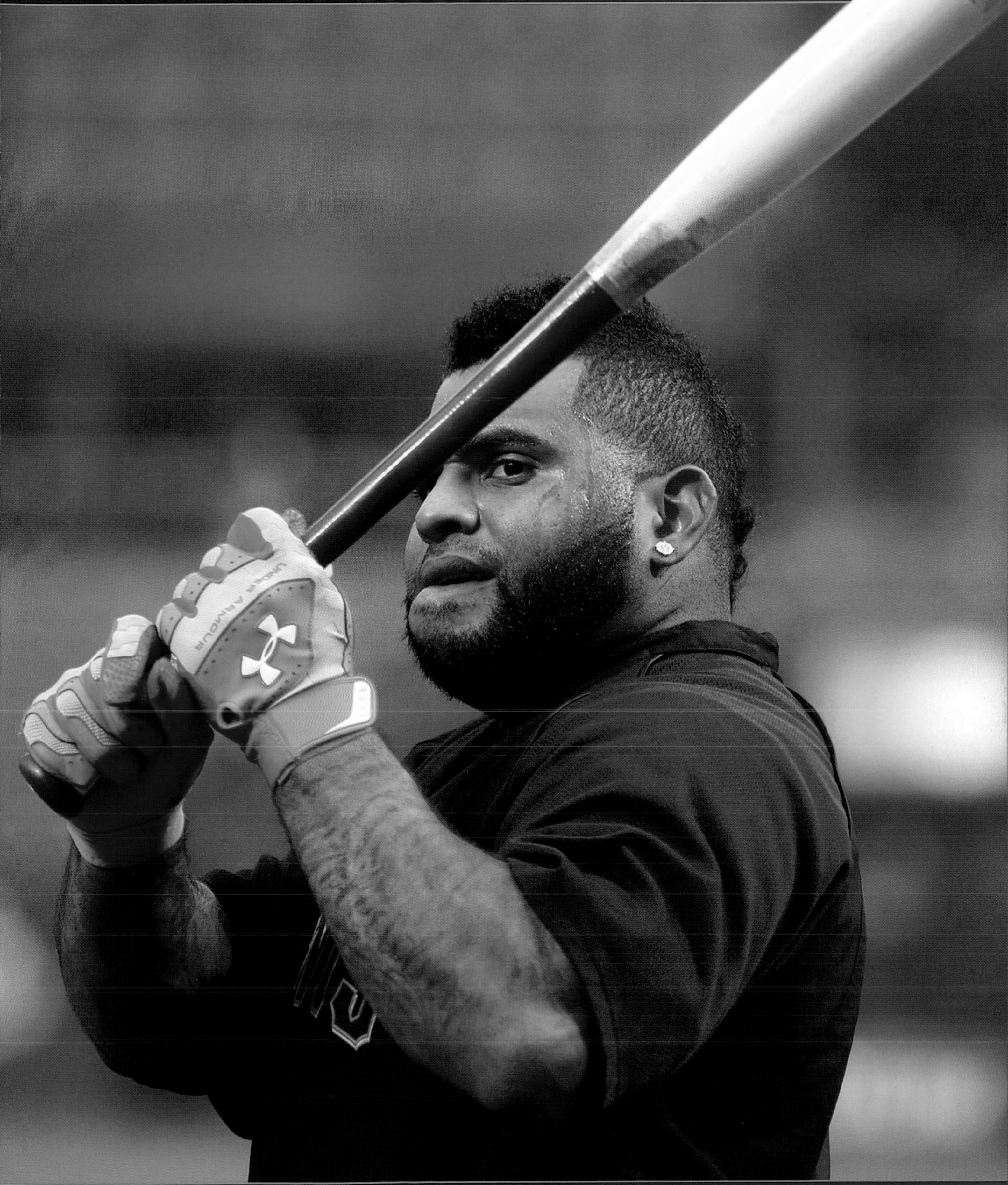
UNDER ARMOUR

consecutive postseason games, a franchise record. He holds the Giants mark with a 14-game postseason hitting streak, a run that included his game-tying double in Game 2 of the N.L. Division Series, a stunning blow to a Washington Nationals team that had gotten 26 outs from Jordan Zimmermann but would lose in 18 innings.

Sandoval, a .325 career hitter in the postseason, also holds the San Francisco Giants record with 11 multi-hit playoff games, including in Thursday's win over St. Louis. With the game tied in the ninth, the Cardinals turned to Michael Wacha for the first time all month. Sandoval didn't walk to the plate dreaming of hitting a walk-off homer; he just wanted to make Wacha uncomfortable. The free-swinging Sandoval looked at a 96 mph first-pitch fastball.

"It was right down the middle, and I took it — I never do that," he said, smiling. "The second pitch was 98, and I fouled it off. After that, I'm like, you know what, just try to put the ball in play and let your teammates take care of everything."

He smoked a changeup for a leadoff single, and Travis Ishikawa took care of the rest, putting Sandoval back in the World Series for a third time.

This run is his most relaxed yet. Sandoval was benched in 2010 and spent much of 2012 thinking about "getting payback for the first one that I didn't play in." Now, he's enjoying the moment — and thriving.

"Great players have a way of elevating their game when the stakes are higher and the stage is bigger, and Pablo certainly seems like one of those players," manager Bruce Bochy said. "He just enjoys it. He's in the moment, but he's excited to be here. You could have a guy go the other way and maybe get a little nervous or whatever, but Pablo, he loves this type of baseball.

"When it gets to this point, he just seems to turn that focus up even more."

Months ago, however, Bochy had to call Sandoval into his office to check on what Sandoval was really focused on. The third baseman finished with a .279 average, 16 homers and 73 RBIs, but that line seemed impossible when he was hitting .173 on May 10. The Giants were worried that Sandoval was thinking too much about his impending contract, and Bochy talked to him about it.

"He's human, and that might have distracted him a little bit," Bochy said. "He assured me, he said: 'I'm not thinking about it. I'll worry about that when the season is over.'"

Sandoval is almost to that point, and while his postseason push will only increase his value, it has put the Giants in a tough spot. They locked up Hunter Pence in the final week of a disappointing 2013 season and signed Tim Lincecum in mid-October when they had exclusive negotiating rights.

Sandoval is mere days away from a market with no shortage of suitors for a 28-year-old who is one of the few impact hitters set to hit free agency and an excellent defender as well. As rumors swirl, the Giants are holding their cards close to the vest, although they will at the very least make Sandoval a qualifying offer of $15.3 million. The offer is unlikely to be accepted.

"We'll address it at the end of the year and see how we'll approach it," general manager Brian Sabean said. "I'm sure [Sandoval's side] has some thoughts, and it takes two to tango."

Sandoval insists he's given no thought to the dance that's waiting whenever the games end. He laughed at the notion of free agency being a distraction this month.

"I still have more games with my teammates. I'm still a Giant," he said. "I don't think about it at all. I want to win the World Series again." ■

SANDOVAL'S PERFORMANCE IN OCTOBER HAS CONTINUED TO STAND OUT THROUGHOUT HIS CAREER. IN GAME 1 OF THE WORLD SERIES, HE NOTCHED A SINGLE, A DOUBLE AND COLLECTED TWO RBIS. (NHAT V. MEYER/STAFF)

GENERAL MANAGER

BRIAN SABEAN

TEAM'S GRIT, PASSION IS A REFLECTION OF GENERAL MANAGER'S ETHOS

BY CARL STEWARD ✦ OCTOBER 21, 2014

KANSAS CITY—The Giants have a leadoff hitter who doesn't hit much, a left fielder who has barely played left field, a lineup that recently went without a home run for 243 at-bats — until its rookie second baseman hit the second one of his career in the game that punched the Giants' ticket to the World Series.

As people attempt to explain how the Giants can be here for the third time in five years, you hear about their pitching, their manager, their defense, their luck. All are valid, to one degree or another.

Often underplayed is their toughness. The Giants are a tough bunch — tough-minded, forged by tough times, tough to beat.

"They are like a bunch of cockroaches," Giants general manager Brian Sabean said after the Giants beat St. Louis in the National League Championship Series. "You gotta kill 'em all off. If you're going to get one, you gotta get 'em all."

Though he wept that night after the victory, Sabean is a tough guy, too. It starts at the top.

LIFE WITH STEINBRENNER

The 58-year-old general manager was a scrappy second baseman at Eckerd College in St. Petersburg, Fla., short on talent but big in heart, according to Steve Balboni. Balboni was a college teammate, a high school rival —

and the starting first baseman for the 1985 World Series champion Kansas City Royals. He's now a scout for the Giants, hired by Sabean in 2009.

"We like to say, 'If the man is equal to his ability, you have a hell of a baseball player,'" said Sabean. "We've got a lot of high-character people, and these guys are tough, tough guys. They're men in every sense of the word, but they play this game with the passion and respect of Little Leaguers. All that's contagious, and that's kind of been the culture we've been able to develop over the years."

"Maybe because he was a scout, it comes from his history of seeing and evaluating players and not only seeing their physical tools, but their mental side," said pitcher Tim Hudson, a tough customer Sabean brought in last winter as a free agent. "Those are the things that general managers can't put a stat on — how tough somebody is, how much guts they have, what kind of chemistry they can bring."

Sabean was a scout for the New York Yankees under George Steinbrenner, an experience that thickened his skin as much as the New Hampshire winters of his youth.

It was Sabean who, in his first act as the Giants GM in 1996, traded fan favorite Matt Williams to Cleveland for Jeff Kent.

GIANTS GENERAL MANAGER BRIAN SABEAN, HIRED IN 1996, IS BASEBALL'S LONGEST-TENURED GENERAL MANAGER. (NHAT V. MEYER/STAFF)

It was Sabean, while with the Yankees, who persuaded Steinbrenner to draft a scrawny high school shortstop from Michigan named Derek Jeter. Sabean also was instrumental in drafting Mariano Rivera, Andy Pettitte and Jorge Posada, cornerstones of the Yankees dynasty and players who represent what Giants manager Bruce Bochy likes to call "championship blood."

"I think Brian looks at building a real team, not just getting the best talent or the guys with good numbers," said Balboni. "Numbers have their place, but it's about finding guys who will help you win. And they have to fit into the atmosphere."

Sabean's most recent acquisition, pitcher Jake Peavy, is a classic example.

While more high-profile pitchers like Jon Lester and David Price were moved at the trade deadline, the Giants zeroed in on a guy who survived a major shoulder injury, a guy who was having a horrible year with the Boston Red Sox, but also a guy they knew had an almost maniacal desire to win, which he exhibits with outbursts of raw emotion every time he takes the mound.

Peavy, 1-9 at time of the trade, went 6-4 for the Giants with a 2.17 ERA. The team won eight of his last nine starts, then won Game 1 of the National League Division Series against Washington behind him.

"You've got to have that drive, that will," said Peavy. "It's as honest and genuine as anything, and it goes beyond the stats.... It is all out of pure motivation of wanting to win, be a part of history, be a champion."

The Giants have a number of players who've been through the brutal grind of just making it to the majors. Pitcher Yusmeiro Petit played in Mexico to keep his dream alive. Ryan Vogelsong had to go to Japan. Travis Ishikawa played in the minors for a number of organizations before hitting the walk-off homer that put the club in the World Series.

"Most of the guys on our team have been through something that made them tougher," said Vogelsong. "There's something that makes you tougher when you get released, or have people tell you the door's closing. It does something to you as a person, and that translates to the baseball field."

"A lot of us were just looking for a place at the table," said Sergio Romo, the undersized reliever who was drafted in the 28th round in 2005, after 851 other players.

'WE'RE NOT THAT TEAM'

Sabean knows he has something special, even if it doesn't glisten in the showroom like more high-priced models that aren't playing for the biggest prize. He knows his team is being sold short and put down — even now — and he couldn't be happier that outsiders still can't figure the Giants out.

"One of the things I believe fuels the fire in these players' bellies is that there's a hell of a lot more talent in that clubhouse than is being given credit for," he said. "It's never been written about, but we have 16 players with World Series rings. We're the farthest thing from the Little Engine That Could. We're not that team."

Indeed, the Giants have talent. And heart. And toughness. It has been the recipe for a 30-11 postseason record since 2010.

Go ahead, tell the Giants they don't belong. They're tough. They can take it, and then prove you wrong. ∎

BRIAN SABEAN HAS FOUND SUCCESS IN DRAFTING PLAYERS WHO FIT INTO THE ATMOSPHERE HE HAS CREATED IN SAN FRANCISCO, NOT JUST THE PLAYERS WITH THE BEST NUMBERS. THAT HAS LED TO CONTINUED POSTSEASON SUCCESS FOR THE FRANCHISE. (D. ROSS CAMERON/STAFF)

NATIONAL LEAGUE
PLAYOFFS

GIANTS' FANS CHEER AS HUNTER
PENCE STEALS SECOND BASE
AGAINST THE CARDINALS IN
GAME 4 OF THE NLCS. PENCE'S
"YES, YES, YES!" BECAME THE
GIANTS' RALLYING CRY IN 2014
(JOSIE LEPE/STAFF)

NATIONAL LEAGUE WILD-CARD GAME
OCTOBER 1, 2014 | GIANTS 8, PIRATES 0

A GRAND OPENING

CRAWFORD'S SLAM, BUMGARNER'S BRILLIANCE VAULT GIANTS TO EASY WILD-CARD WIN

BY ALEX PAVLOVIC

PITTSBURGH—The chants were deafening and in unison. "Ed-die! Ed-die! Ed-die!"

With one swing of Brandon Crawford's bat, 40,000 voices gave way to silence.

Crawford became the first shortstop in MLB history to hit a postseason grand slam, and Madison Bumgarner did the rest in an 8-0 win over the Pittsburgh Pirates that sent the Giants from a winner-takes-all wild-card game to a National League Division Series matchup with the Washington Nationals.

Once Crawford's shot off Edinson Volquez cleared the right field wall, the Giants dugout knew the game was over. Crawford wasn't even thinking about hitting a grand slam. He didn't think Bumgarner needed that much help.

"With Madison out there looking as sharp as he did, you figured only one run could do it," he said.

It would have. Bumgarner threw just 109 pitches while becoming the first Giant since Tim Lincecum in 2010 to throw a postseason shutout. He gave the kind of performance you would expect from a wunderkind who first dominated the postseason at the age of 21, striking out 10 and allowing only four hits. The lineup nearly matched that in the decisive rally.

The Pirates gambled on Sunday and threw Gerrit Cole at the Cincinnati Reds in a last-ditch effort to win the National League Central. Cole struck out 12, but the Pirates dropped the game, and thus it was the talented but unpredictable Volquez who took the ball. The Giants felt they were seeing his pitches well early on, and they finally broke through in the fourth.

Pablo Sandoval led off and poked a low two-strike curveball into right field for his second hit. Hunter Pence bounced one through the left side of the infield, and Brandon Belt spat on a good 2-2 slider and ended up walking to load the bases.

Crawford has a history of clearing the bags in big moments in his career. While playing for the San Jose Giants in 2010, Crawford hit an extra-innings grand slam to spark a win in Game 3 of the California League Championship Series. A year later, he hit a go-ahead slam against the Milwaukee Brewers in his MLB debut. None of those past moments were on his mind as he dug in with PNC Park shaking around him.

"The last thing I was thinking about was hitting a homer," he said, smiling.

Crawford was looking for a pitch he could drive deep enough to score Sandoval. Volquez was looking for

BRANDON CRAWFORD HITS A GRAND SLAM IN THE FOURTH INNING, BECOMING THE FIRST SHORTSTOP TO DO SO IN THE POSTSEASON. (AP IMAGES)

one he could bury. The curveball hung, and on a still night along the Allegheny River, Crawford left no doubt about where this one would land.

He had seen that kind of suction in a stadium before, and thought back to Game 5 of the NLDS in 2012, when Sergio Romo won a tense battle with the Reds' Jay Bruce and Great American Ball Park deflated.

"When I hit it, it died down a little bit," he said. "Then it went over the fence, and it was just silent."

There is no better feeling for a visiting team than to be the only ones making noise in a ballpark, and as Crawford headed down the steps, the Giants breathed a sigh of relief. They had seen this Bumgarner before, and it didn't take long for it to become apparent that he wasn't going to let the season end.

Bumgarner didn't go to a two-ball count until the 10th Pirates batter of the game, and he needed just 28 pitches — 23 of them strikes — to get through the first three innings.

"I don't say it much, but in the bullpen he just had that feel," catcher Buster Posey said. "He threw the ball where he wanted to. The moment never seemed too big for him."

Bumgarner said he was calm in the hours leading up to the 8:09 p.m. first pitch. He ordered room service and refused to let the magnitude of the moment overwhelm him.

"I took the day real slow," he said. "That's what I like to do."

Deliberately and methodically, he picked the Pirates apart. The Giants kept adding on, with Belt driving in three runs he knew Bumgarner wouldn't need.

"I don't know if it's a good thing for him, but we all expected him to come out and do what he did tonight," Belt said. "When he takes the mound, he rises to the occasion. It was unbelievable. It was so loud, and it didn't bother him at all."

Bumgarner and Crawford made sure the noise was a footnote, not a soundtrack.

"It was an up-and-down season all year for us, but once we get to the playoffs, it's a new season," Crawford said. "That probably has a lot to do with the character of this team. We all just come together and battle." ■

THIRD BASEMAN PABLO SANDOVAL FLIPS OVER THE DUGOUT RAILING TO CATCH A FOUL BALL IN THE SEVENTH INNING. (AP IMAGES)

NATIONAL LEAGUE DIVISION SERIES: GAME 1
OCTOBER 3, 2014 | GIANTS 3, NATIONALS 2

BACK TO BUSINESS

UNDERDOG GIANTS WIN 9TH IN ROW IN POSTSEASON

BY ALEX PAVLOVIC

WASHINGTON—The Giants are underdogs once again. They're missing their best right-handed starter, their leadoff hitter and their left fielder, and they're facing the best team in the National League.

It's a situation that seemed to call for an inspirational pregame speech from Hunter Pence, and maybe a sunflower seed shower or two in the dugout. You know, just to rekindle that "backs against the wall" magic that worked so well in 2012. And yet, the dugout floor was clean after a 3-2 win Friday over the Washington Nationals in Game 1 of the best-of-five N.L. Division Series. Pence's voice was full and cheery, not hoarse.

"I don't think there was any need for it," first baseman Brandon Belt said. "We knew the deal coming into this series."

And they didn't care.

Everyone can call them the underdogs, and the Giants do, too. But they prefer another October tag: unbeatable. The two-time champs have won nine straight in the playoffs and 23 of 31 dating to 2010.

"You know," manager Bruce Bochy said, "they've got a calmness about them."

That paid off early on an overcast day at Nationals Park. Stephen Strasburg lit up the radar gun and Jake Peavy painted the corners, and in time, the artist won.

Peavy allowed just two hits in 5⅔ shutout innings, getting his first postseason win.

This group has vanquished all kinds of pitchers in October, but few if any have possessed the raw stuff of Strasburg. He threw nine fastballs in a perfect first inning, all at 97 mph or above and the final one clocking in at 99 mph. It was Strasburg's fastest pitch in two years and got a flyout from Buster Posey, the third of the inning.

It was an overpowering display, and in the dugout the Giants had the same thought. We're going to get him.

"It was kind of like the (wild-card) game in Pittsburgh. You could see right away that people were having good at-bats," Belt said. "You could kind of tell a little bit that guys had a good chance at hitting him, and we did."

The Giants struck in the third inning, when Travis Ishikawa hit a leadoff single and reached second as first baseman Adam LaRoche made a late throw on Peavy's bunt. Joe Panik lined a single to center two batters later, picking up his first postseason RBI.

Hunter Pence made it 2-0 with a manufactured rally in the fourth. He beat out the second throw on a would-be double-play grounder to short and then saw an opening and stole second. Belt followed with a single to right, and Pence scored easily.

Strasburg wouldn't make it out of the sixth, giving

ROOKIE INFIELDER JOE PANIK HITS A TRIPLE IN THE SEVENTH INNING OF GAME 1. (NHAT V. MEYER/STAFF)

up eight hits — all singles — and two runs. In his last two starts against the Giants, Strasburg has recorded just 27 outs and given up 16 hits. Bochy was pleased with the lineup's approach against so many fastballs that registered in the upper 90s.

"I don't think you ever change from trying to get a good pitch to hit," he said. "That's the way it should be. Don't try to do too much. Don't overanalyze anything. You start thinking too much against a good pitcher, and you get yourself in trouble. We try to keep it simple."

Peavy did the same, but in a much different way. He piled up a high pitch count, but that was by design. Peavy wasn't going to give this deep Nationals lineup anything that could be shot over a wall, and he worked the corners at will.

"They didn't give anything away," he said. "They didn't give any at-bats away."

Peavy didn't allow many of them to end successfully for the Nationals. They didn't have a hit through four innings, but a Nate Schierholtz double and walk of Jayson Werth put Peavy in a tight spot in the sixth. Javier Lopez entered to face LaRoche and walked him, loading the bases.

In the most important spot of the season thus far, Bochy turned to rookie Hunter Strickland, a September call-up. Strickland got the first two strikes on Ian Desmond with three big fastballs: 99 mph, 98 mph, 99 mph. The fourth postseason pitch of Strickland's big league career was a 100 mph heater that Desmond swung through, getting the Giants out of the jam.

"He stepped right into as big a fire as you could step into and he came up huge for us," Pence said. "It was really amazing and impressive."

Strickland didn't give up a run in nine September appearances, but Bryce Harper got to him in the seventh, crushing a 97 mph fastball into the upper deck in right. Asdrubal Cabrera homered two batters later, but the Giants still held the lead thanks to Panik's insurance run in the top of the inning. As they always seem to do this time of year, the Giants held on, throwing an early body blow at a Nationals team that won a league-best 96 games.

"We understand that we might not be man for man, you know, the favorites," Peavy said. "We are not given a lot of credit. We take pride in being chained together. Our strength is in who we are as a team."

More often than not, that's the team smiling after the final pitch. ∎

ABOVE: CENTER FIELDER GREGOR BLANCO LEAVES HIS FEET TO SNAG A FLY BALL HIT BY THE NATIONALS' ADAM LAROCHE. (NHAT V. MEYER/STAFF) OPPOSITE: AFTER TAGGING OUT BRYCE HARPER, BRANDON CRAWFORD THROWS TO FIRST BASE TO COMPLETE A FIFTH-INNING DOUBLE PLAY. (NHAT V. MEYER/STAFF)

THE LONGEST GAME

HOME RUN IN 18TH INNING GIVES GIANTS 2-0 LEAD IN SERIES

BY ALEX PAVLOVIC

WASHINGTON—With one quick flick of the bat, Brandon Belt ended a historic filibuster at Nationals Park.

Belt's 18th-inning blast gave the Giants a gripping 2-1 win over the Washington Nationals in the longest game in postseason history, a 6-hour, 23-minute epic that was the Jordan Zimmermann show for the first three hours and Yusmeiro Petit's masterpiece for most of the next three.

Zimmermann was one out away from a shutout that would have tied this best-of-five National League Division Series, but he was pulled after a walk of Joe Panik and could only watch as Pablo Sandoval drove in the tying run. Petit would keep the game even with six innings of one-hit, seven-strikeout dominance in extra innings, repeatedly setting a stage that Belt finally jumped on in the 18th.

"I'm delirious," Belt said. "I'm just trying to soak it all in. It was awesome, it was fun — I don't even know what to say. I can't even think straight, to be honest with you. It's all a blur."

That was just fine, actually. This story was better told by items, like the pitching machine Belt wore out in the final weeks of the season as he frantically tried to recover from a concussion and find his swing in time for the playoffs. That machine can get cranked up to about 94 mph, and with Belt's bat looking slow, hitting coach Hensley Meulens had Belt cut the distance from machine to plate in half, taking swings from 30 feet away.

"He's worked hard to get to this point," Meulens said. "He had to pick up his hand speed, because it wasn't there when he came back in September. When you have natural strength like he does, all you have to do is catch the ball out front and it tends to go a long way."

Before Belt could catch Tanner Roark's fastball on the sweet spot, however, the Giants had to find a way to extend their night. That seemed nearly impossible against Zimmermann, even with Tim Hudson matching him step for step. Hudson stumbled just once, giving up a third-inning run. Zimmermann fed off the lead, getting through eight innings on just 88 pitches.

Zimmermann threw a no-hitter on the final day of the regular season, and on this night he was nearly as overpowering, retiring 20 straight before Panik's two-out walk. It was at that point that first-year manager Matt Williams made a call that will be scrutinized all winter in the nation's capital if his team can't find a way to recover. Zimmermann had thrown 100 pitches, but he was pulled for closer Drew Storen, who coughed up the lead on back-to-back hits from Buster Posey and Sandoval. Williams said he had no intention of letting Zimmermann face Posey, who had lined out to third in his previous at-bat.

JEREMY AFFELDT CELEBRATES AFTER PITCHING THE FINAL OUT OF THE 10TH INNING OF GAME 2. AFFELDT WAS ONE OF SEVEN GIANTS RELIEVERS TO PITCH IN THE 18-INNING CONTEST. (NHAT V. MEYER/STAFF)

"Hindsight is a great thing," he said. "You know, if our starting pitcher goes out there, and he's at 100 pitches the third time, fourth time through the lineup, and he gets in trouble in the ninth, we will go to the guy who has been perfect for us since he has been in that role. It didn't work out."

Williams was fine with his decision. So, too, were the Giants.

"I was pretty happy he wasn't out there anymore," Hudson said of Zimmermann. "They could have brought Sandy Koufax in and we probably would have had smiles on our faces."

Hudson went from starter to cheerleader after Sandoval's big at-bat, and he was joined by a growing cast of relievers. Five pitchers helped bridge the gap from Hudson to Petit, who threw 80 pitches out of the bullpen, just 17 fewer than Hudson had thrown. Like Petit, Roark had a strong season in the rotation only to be pushed to the bullpen by the postseason.

As Belt prepared for the hard-throwing right-hander, he turned to an item as trustworthy to him as that pitching machine: A sugar-free Red Bull. The light blue and silver can is never far from Belt's locker, but he wasn't the only one reloading as a game that started at 5:38 p.m. locally inched past midnight. Sandoval munched on a protein bar in the dugout. Hunter Strickland and Tim Lincecum, the last two left in the bullpen, shared snacks and huddled near a heater on a chilly night, watching as Petit kept churning along.

They all learned later that they had played in the second game in postseason history to reach the 18th inning. Belt mercifully ended it, reaching the second deck on a night when sluggers Bryce Harper, Adam LaRoche and Posey had failed to cut through the wind with hard-hit balls.

"He's the strongest," Meulens said, laughing. "That one just had a different sound to it."

It shouldn't have been an unfamiliar one, though. As Belt dramatically dropped his bat and the visiting dugout exploded, a number popped up on the scoreboard's radar gun, one Belt has come to know all too well.

Roark's pitch had come in at 94 mph. ■

BRANDON BELT BLASTS THE GAME-WINNING HOME RUN OVER THE RIGHT FIELD WALL IN THE TOP OF THE 18TH INNING. GAME 2 OF THE NLDS SPANNED SIX HOURS, 23 MINUTES. (NHAT V. MEYER/STAFF)

WITH TWO OUTS IN THE NINTH
INNING OF GAME 2, PABLO
SANDOVAL HITS AN RBI DOUBLE,
DRIVING IN JOE PANIK TO TIE THE
GAME. (NHAT V. MEYER/STAFF)

NATIONAL LEAGUE DIVISION SERIES: GAME 3

OCTOBER 6, 2014 | NATIONALS 4, GIANTS 1

AN OH-NO THROW

AIDED BY BUMGARNER'S ERRANT TOSS, NATIONALS STAY ALIVE

BY ALEX PAVLOVIC

SAN FRANCISCO—When it was over, the Giants could look back on a 10-game postseason winning streak with pride. It spanned three series and a wild-card game over two postseasons and set a National League record.

The streak included plenty of plays like the decisive one Monday. This time, however, the Giants were the ones to compound the mental mistake with a physical one, and it cost them in a 4-1 loss to the Washington Nationals.

Madison Bumgarner's throw in a key seventh-inning moment skipped into left field, and as the ball bounced off the rolled-up tarp and over the bullpen mound, the game spun away, too. Two runs scored, and the Nationals wouldn't look back, winning behind Doug Fister and cutting the Giants' lead in the National League Division Series to 2-1.

The pressure is on the Giants, as they learned in 2012, when they overcame a 2-0 deficit against the Cincinnati Reds. You put a team away when you have the chance, and the Giants didn't.

"We know how good this club is that we're playing," manager Bruce Bochy said. "You have to play your best ball to beat them. Today we didn't, and we made a mistake that hurt us."

Actually, it was two mistakes on the same play.

Bumgarner and Fister had cruised through most of a rematch of Game 2 of the 2012 World Series, when Fister was a Tiger, and the game was scoreless entering the seventh. But the Nationals got going with an Ian Desmond single and Bryce Harper walk to open the inning. Slow-footed catcher Wilson Ramos had not laid down a sacrifice bunt in three years, but eager to stay out of a double play and advance the go-ahead run to third, the Nationals put the bunt on and kept it on even as Ramos fell behind 1-2.

Bumgarner threw a slider across the outside corner, and Ramos tapped it perfectly, dropping it between the mound and the first-base line. Even at 6-foot-5, 235 pounds, Bumgarner is a good athlete and nimble fielder. He bounced off the mound and scooped the ball up as catcher Buster Posey screamed to cut off the lead runner at third.

"Oh, lord," Ramos said to himself as Posey yelled. He was afraid he had just bunted into a double play, but Bumgarner's throw was so far to the left of Pablo Sandoval that he couldn't get a glove on it, and it skipped away from the infield as left fielder Travis Ishikawa gave chase. Desmond scored easily, and Harper came around all the way from first.

"I thought I might have had a shot," Bumgarner said. "Regardless of whether I get (Desmond) out or

GREGOR BLANCO WALKS OFF THE FIELD AFTER LINING OUT IN THE EIGHTH INNING OF GAME 3. THE LOSS TO THE NATIONALS ENDED THE GIANTS' 10-GAME POSTSEASON WINNING STREAK. (NHAT V. MEYER/STAFF)

The two-run hole would become three before a stunned sellout crowd could fully comprehend what had just happened. Asdrubal Cabrera poked a bouncer into left, and Ramos made good on Nationals third-base coach Bob Henley's aggressive send, scoring just ahead of Ishikawa's throw home.

Fister, a Merced native, gave up just one run in that 2012 matchup but took a crushing loss. He wouldn't bend this time.

The Giants had a couple of early chances as Fister knocked the rust off after a 10-day layoff, getting two runners on with one out in the second. But Harper made a leaping catch on the warning track on a drive hit by Brandon Crawford, and after a walk of Ishikawa, Fister threw a two-seamer past Bumgarner, who had two grand slams in the regular season.

Harper homered in the top of the ninth, and Drew Storen — who blew Game 2 — held on after putting the first two runners on. As the Giants watched another team enjoy a postseason handshake line for the first time since Game 4 of the 2012 NLCS, the late afternoon sun shined light on a troubling fact. The Giants are hitting .208 through three games, and they've scored just six runs.

"They really do have some tremendous arms, and you understand that when you're going to play these guys," right fielder Hunter Pence said. "They also play tremendous defense. That's a good combination.... The story has yet to be written. A lot of times you don't remember the games in the middle. You remember the clinch game." ∎

not, I felt we still had a shot at getting Ramos at first. But I can't throw the ball away right there, obviously. I shouldn't have done that. Regardless of whether I should have thrown over there or not, I can't throw that ball away."

Bumgarner regretted the physical act. Posey regretted his decision.

"I just thought the way it jumped off the bat, we might have had a shot," he said. "But Desmond had a good jump. We probably should have just taken the out at first."

ABOVE: GIANTS STARTER MADISON BUMGARNER TALKS TO PITCHING COACH DAVE RIGHETTI AND CATCHER BUSTER POSEY AFTER TWO NATIONALS SCORED ON BUMGARNER'S SEVENTH-INNING THROWING ERROR. (NHAT V. MEYER/ STAFF) OPPOSITE: GREGOR BLANCO EXTENDS TO CATCH A FLY BALL OFF THE BAT OF THE NATIONALS' WILSON RAMOS IN THE NINTH INNING. (JOSE CARLOS FAJARDO/STAFF)

NATIONAL LEAGUE DIVISION SERIES: GAME 4
OCTOBER 7, 2014 | GIANTS 3, NATIONALS 2

YES! YES! YES!

S.F. SCRATCHES OUT GAME 4 WIN

BY ALEX PAVLOVIC

SAN FRANCISCO—Before the wild-card game in Pittsburgh, Giants closer Santiago Casilla saw Mike Krukow in the PNC Park dugout and pointed at the World Series ring on the broadcaster's finger.

"One more," Casilla said firmly, a steely look in his eyes.

When Casilla threw the final shutout inning of the National League Division Series, the Giants were one step closer to that next ring, having defeated the favored Washington Nationals 3-2 to take the series in four and advance to the NLCS for the third time in five seasons. Led by a brilliant starting staff, the Giants held a 96-win team to nine runs in four games, setting up another matchup with the St. Louis Cardinals.

Ryan Vogelsong picked up the baton, wiping away what he felt was a disappointing regular season with 5⅓ strong innings. Vogelsong has a 1.19 ERA in five career postseason starts. He's the first starting pitcher in major league history to allow one run or fewer in each of his first five postseason starts.

"I just love it, man. I love it," he said. "This is what you play the game for in your backyard when you're throwing the ball off the wall. You pretend you're in this situation. I love playoff baseball, I love the pressure, and I love the high stress situations.

"Somehow, I've been blessed, and I get it done."

Vogelsong had a 5.53 ERA in September and 4.00 ERA for the season, but the Giants knew early Tuesday that he would be a different guy in the clincher. Catcher Buster Posey heard his glove popping a little louder in the bullpen.

"I could tell the fastball had a lot of life," Posey said. "Although I wouldn't have guessed it was 95. It's funny what adrenaline can do for you."

In his first inning since Sept. 26, Vogelsong twice hit 95 mph with his fastball. They were his hardest pitches since the 2012 postseason, and all around the field Vogelsong's teammates tried to stifle grins. Back-up catcher Andrew Susac looked at stunned teammates in the dugout and all wondered how much adrenaline was coursing through Vogelsong's 37-year-old body. At shortstop, Brandon Crawford looked up, saw the radar gun and thought, "This is what he does for us." Across the diamond, Brandon Belt had a different thought.

"Who said he was old?" he said, laughing.

Vogelsong said he made mechanical adjustments over the past week to get "through the ball better" and get rid of a flaw that was zapping his power. After that, the atmosphere took over. Adrenaline only carries you so far, though, especially when you're looking at

SLAMMING INTO THE RIGHT FIELD WALL, HUNTER PENCE ROBS JAYSON WERTH OF EXTRA BASES IN THE SIXTH INNING OF GAME 4. (D. ROSS CAMERON/STAFF)

a cross-country trip for Game 5. Before any tightness could settle into the Giants' limbs, they found a way to scratch across two runs.

Crawford hit a one-out liner off Gio Gonzalez in the second, and the left-hander flubbed Juan Perez's tapper back to the mound, putting a second runner on. Vogelsong tried to move both runners over and also ended up reaching when Gonzalez and third baseman Anthony Rendon called each other off on a perfect bunt down the third-base line.

With the bases loaded, Gonzalez walked Gregor Blanco on four pitches. Crawford jogged home as Blanco stood at the plate for a second, clapping his hands in the direction of a boisterous Giants dugout. Earlier, he had told Hunter Pence that the Giants — without Angel Pagan and Michael Morse — had to find a way to win ugly.

"Let's do it the best, ugliest way we can do it," he said. "We have great defense and great pitching, so we just need to get timely hits and do the little things. We know we're not the best-hitting team in baseball, but we can play together. If we've got to steal the game, we're going to do it."

Rookie second baseman Joe Panik stole another run after falling behind 0-2. He had grounded out to the right side five straight times over two games, but with a runner on third, he knew all he had to do was put the ball in play. A grounder to first scored another run.

Vogelsong had a no-hitter until the fifth, when a single by Ian Desmond and double by Bryce Harper got the Nationals within one. Adrenaline gave way to fatigue, but with his fastball down to the upper 80s in the sixth, Vogelsong got a boost from the most adrenaline-filled player in orange and black.

Pence grew up with a Michael Jordan "Jumpman" poster on his wall, and when Jayson Werth crushed a liner to right, Pence imitated the pose while making an incredible catch as he slammed back first into a chain-link fence.

"I never do anything cool," Pence said. "So this is weird for me."

It was a relief for Vogelsong, but soon the game would be tied. Harper hit a moonshot into McCovey Cove off Hunter Strickland in the seventh, but again the Giants bounced right off the mat. Panik and Posey singled with one down in the bottom of the inning, and Pence walked to load the bases. A wild pitch scored the final run of the NLDS.

Sergio Romo and Casilla made it hold up, clinching another celebration for a group that's gotten used to this. After vanquishing the deep Nationals, the Giants looked ahead to a rematch of the 2012 NLCS, one won in seven games. Vogelsong started two of those, and in this series he helped the rotation fashion a 1.04 ERA over four starts.

As Vogelsong led the Giants in a "Yes! Yes! Yes!" chant that's become tradition, general manager Brian Sabean slipped in and out of clubhouse corners, offering handshakes to players who refused to give in once again.

"It's a will to win. A will to win," he said, proudly surveying the scene. "They compete better than anybody in almost any sport. They just keep playing. I can't explain it." ∎

GIANTS PLAYERS AND FANS CELEBRATE THE NLDS-CLINCHING GAME 4 VICTORY THAT PROPELLED THE GIANTS INTO THE NATIONAL LEAGUE CHAMPIONSHIP SERIES AGAINST THE CARDINALS. (D. ROSS CAMERON/STAFF)

NATIONAL LEAGUE CHAMPIONSHIP SERIES: GAME 1
OCTOBER 11, 2014 | GIANTS 3, CARDINALS 0

PUTTING ON THE PRESSURE

UNYIELDING GIANTS BLANK CARDINALS IN SERIES OPENER

BY ALEX PAVLOVIC

ST. LOUIS—The Giants don't know quite how to explain this, either, except to point at the calendar.

The lineup that went down so easily in the middle of the summer is now a grinding October machine, piecing odd rallies together and wearing down one big name after the next. Saturday's punching bag was Adam Wainwright, with the perennial Cy Young Award contender lasting just 4⅔ innings before being lifted in a 3–0 Giants win that gave them an early lead over the St. Louis Cardinals in this N. L. Championship Series.

Join the list of the weary, Adam. It grows by the day.

Edinson Volquez and Stephen Strasburg? Done without recording an out in the sixth inning. Gio Gonzalez? He lasted just four innings in the final game of the NLDS. All this against a lineup that ranked 11th in the National League in pitches per plate appearance during the regular season while following a simple credo: Be aggressive, look for your pitch, and put a good swing on it.

Yet there was Wainwright, 69 pitches down after three and taxed by 98 pitches by the time he was knocked out in the fifth.

"That's what you have to do in the postseason," said first baseman Brandon Belt, who walked twice and singled. "When you're facing pitchers like this, you can't go after their pitch. We go out there with the approach that if we're going to get out, we're going to get out on our terms." It sounds simple, and yet it's not for others. The Cardinals saw 126 pitches while getting shut out by Madison Bumgarner, Sergio Romo and Santiago Casilla. The lineup that twice stunned surefire Cy Young winner Clayton Kershaw had just four hits against Bumgarner and struck out seven times.

"When he's throwing the ball as well as he was tonight, you know you don't need to score many runs," catcher Buster Posey said.

The Giants got three in the first three innings against Wainwright, wearing him out with a 36-pitch second inning that was fueled by Cardinals mistakes. After the teams spent two days at Busch Stadium telling reporters that they were similar, that they made the right play and didn't make mistakes, the Cardinals seized up. Randal Grichuk had a bead on Pablo Sandoval's leadoff liner in the second but dropped it as he bounced off the right field fence. Wainwright walked Hunter Pence, and then Belt dumped a 2-2 cutter into left field. After a strikeout by Brandon

BRANDON BELT HITS A SACRIFICE FLY TO SCORE BUSTER POSEY IN THE THIRD INNING. THE GIANTS' FIRST BASEMAN NOTCHED A HIT, SACRIFICE FLY AND TWO WALKS IN GAME 1. (NHAT V. MEYER/STAFF)

Crawford, Travis Ishikawa sliced a blooper down the left-field line, scoring an early run.

It was the first postseason RBI in four years for the 31-year-old starting in the outfield for just the eighth time in his career.

Afterward, Ishikawa admitted that he thought seriously about spending this fall kicking off retirement, not a postseason rally. He saw his family for just 14 days from Feb. 1 to Sept. 1 of last season while toiling away in the minors, but the Giants gave him a second chance this April.

Even with Michael Morse back on the active roster, manager Bruce Bochy stuck with Ishikawa. That confidence surged through his bat and rarely used outfield glove on a night when he singled twice and made a diving catch in left field.

"There's just something about his gut and his instincts," Ishikawa said. "He finds a way to put you in the best possible situation to succeed."

Bochy tries that at all times, but it doesn't always work. The Giants slumped through much of the summer but have been unyielding in October. They had six hits off Wainwright and felt the score could have, and should have, been lopsided.

"I don't know how to explain it," Ishikawa said. "In the postseason, guys just find a second gear. We bear down and put together good at-bats."

Posey put it another way.

"We put pressure on the other team," he said.

The Cardinals cracked. Ishikawa's single extended a rally that would continue when Matt Carpenter booted Gregor Blanco's two-out grounder to third. Another run scored as a weary Wainwright looked on in disbelief.

"They capitalized," Cardinals manager Mike Matheny said. "It was going to be that kind of game and that kind of series."

The Giants cashed in on another mistake an inning later. Kolten Wong bobbled Pence's grounder that looked like a tailor-made double play, so Posey reached third with one out, not two. That meant Belt's fly ball to center scored a run instead of ending the inning.

The third run was nice, but unnecessary. Bumgarner ran into trouble only once, when he put two on with one out in the seventh. He beat Wong to the bag on a grounder, throwing a body blow along with the tag. The third out was a 93 mph fastball thrown past pinch-hitter Tony Cruz.

Bumgarner has allowed just 14 hits and two earned runs in 23⅔ innings this October. He set an MLB postseason record by extending his scoreless streak on the road to 26⅔ innings.

"You know, that's pretty cool obviously to have any kind of record," he said, "But there are stats for everything nowadays."

There are, and sometimes they lie. Just ask the four starters who are wondering how the supposedly free-swinging Giants offense put such a beating on their arms. ∎

ABOVE: MADISON BUMGARNER REACTS AFTER EXITING THE GAME IN THE EIGHTH INNING. BUMGARNER STRUCK OUT SEVEN CARDINALS IN 7 ⅔ INNINGS. (NHAT V. MEYER/STAFF) OPPOSITE: GIANTS CENTER FIELDER GREGOR BLANCO MAKES A RUNNING CATCH IN THE FIRST INNING. (NHAT V. MEYER/STAFF)

NATIONAL LEAGUE CHAMPIONSHIP SERIES: GAME 2
OCTOBER 12, 2014 | CARDINALS 5, GIANTS 4

ONE FOR THE BIRDS

CARDINALS SHOCK GIANTS WITH FOUR HOMERS

BY ALEX PAVLOVIC

ST. LOUIS—Might beat fight at Busch Stadium on Sunday night.

The Giants scratched across runs on a ground out, two singles and a wild pitch. The Cardinals countered with four homers, the final one a Kolten Wong walk-off in the bottom of the ninth that clinched a 5-4 Cardinals win in Game 2 and evened the N. L. Championship Series.

"The long ball got us," manager Bruce Bochy said.

And it kept the Cardinals alive on a night when they blew a late lead and lost star catcher Yadier Molina to a strained oblique for the rest of the series. The homers were a shock to the system for all involved. The Cardinals ranked last in the National League with 105 homers during the regular season, and the Giants bullpen allowed just 35 in 472 innings.

But in three consecutive innings late Sunday, three different Cardinals homered off three Giants relievers, including Sergio Romo, who spent much of the spring preparing for this very moment. What happened?

"Changeup," he said quickly of his pitch to Wong. "Down the middle."

It's the pitch Romo spent much of the spring refining, so much so that there was concern that he was hurt when he ditched his trademark slider during one brutal Cactus League outing after another. Romo insisted he was looking at the big picture, trying to add a third option that could neutralize left-handers.

"I worked on it so I could better my arsenal, so I could better myself," he said Sunday. "I felt that was one of the things I needed to work on."

Romo threw the pitch 90 times this season, more than the past three seasons combined, and gave up just a lone single and a double. But Wong hit this one like he knew it was coming, leading off the bottom of the ninth with a screamer down the right field line that landed in the first row of seats. Romo said his changeup was diving in the bullpen.

"I went in there confident in it," he said. "Did I expect to throw it down the middle? No chance."

As they packed for a return trip home, the Giants spent much of their time wondering how their bullpen had been so thoroughly ambushed. Rookie pinch-hitter Oscar Taveras tied the game in the seventh by crushing a Jean Machi changeup that was supposed to be in the dirt but instead sat on a tee. With the game still knotted at three in the eighth, Matt Adams crushed a 97 mph fastball from Hunter Strickland. It was the fourth homer allowed by Strickland this postseason, all to left-handed hitters.

"I'd love to ask Adams if he was just sold out on the

STARTER JAKE PEAVY DELIVERS A PITCH IN THE FIRST INNING. PEAVY ALLOWED FOUR HITS IN FOUR INNINGS IN GAME 2. (NHAT V. MEYER/STAFF)

Randal Grichuk and a grand escape by Peavy, who was allowed to face Carpenter with the bases loaded and Javier Lopez warming up in the bullpen. He got a fly out.

Bochy kept showing that faith in his system throughout the night, sometimes getting burned and sometimes getting by. The Giants scored in the fifth on Joaquin Arias' ground out and added runs the next two innings on singles by Hunter Pence and Gregor Blanco. The bullpen kept giving it back, but Bochy turned to his kids in the ninth and was rewarded.

With the Giants trailing after Adams' homer, rookie Andrew Susac ignited a rally with a one-out single off Cardinals closer Trevor Rosenthal. Bochy has steadfastly stood behind slumping outfielder Juan Perez, and his single moved pinch-runner Matt Duffy up to second with one out. With two down, rookie Joe Panik fell behind 0-2 but worked a nail-biting walk. Rosenthal's fourth ball spiked in the dirt in front of the plate and bounced away from Tony Cruz, in for the injured Molina. Duffy, in his third month in the big leagues, raced around safely from second.

"I saw the ball bounce off the dirt, and my first instinct was to go," he said. "(Third-base coach Tim) Flannery was waving me, too. I guess it was instincts."

Wong is just as baby-faced as the Giants' late-season saviors, and the 24-year-old showed some good instincts of his own in the bottom of the inning. As he walked to the plate, A.J. Pierzynski, the former Giant and current backup to Molina and Cruz, told Wong to think about a base hit, not a homer. Wong ignored him.

After he crossed the plate, Wong quickly found Pierzynski.

"Did I get on base?" he playfully yelled.

Unfortunately for the Giants, he got all four of them. ■

heater," catcher Buster Posey said. "That's impressive after three breaking balls that he could get on top of it."

Adams, the 260-pound first baseman nicknamed Big City, said the Cardinals are just keeping it simple.

"You know, we're just going up there barreling balls up, staying through the ball and getting that backspin to carry," he said. "Throughout the season people were worried about our power, but we knew inside the clubhouse that we didn't lose any power."

That showed even against the Giants' starter, Jake Peavy. He lasted just four innings, giving up a solo shot to Matt Carpenter and a second run during a long fourth inning that included a surprise bunt by Molina, an intentional walk of Wong, an RBI single by rookie

HUNTER STRICKLAND CAN ONLY WATCH AS THE CARDINALS' MATT ADAMS CIRCLES THE BASES AFTER ADAMS' EIGHTH-INNING HOME RUN. ADAMS' SHOT GAVE THE CARDINALS A 4-3 LEAD. (NHAT V. MEYER/STAFF)

PINCH HITTER MICHAEL MORSE BREAKS HIS BAT IN THE SEVENTH INNING. MORSE COLLECTED AN INFIELD HIT IN HIS ONLY PLATE APPEARANCE IN GAME 2. (NHAT V. MEYER/STAFF)

A WIN IS A WIN

GIANTS BEAT CARDINALS ON ERROR IN 10TH

BY ALEX PAVLOVIC

SAN FRANCISCO—There are bundles of statistics in the Giants clubhouse, sitting on the manager's desk and in backrooms and on chairs alongside lockers. You can find a number for anything.

But it's October, and these are the Giants. Throw out the numbers, the odds and conventional wisdom.

They find some way to win, and on Tuesday it was another strange one. Randy Choate threw Gregor Blanco's sacrifice bunt down the right-field line in the 10th inning, and Brandon Crawford raced home, clinching a 5-4 win over the St. Louis Cardinals in Game 3 of the N. L. Championship Series.

The Giants lead the series 2-1 after becoming the first National League team to win a postseason game on a walk-off error since Bill Buckner's famous flub in the 1986 World Series.

"Rocks and slingshots, man," third base coach Tim Flannery said, smiling and shaking his head. "We can score runs without hits. We've proven that."

They do it better than anybody this time of year.

The Giants have fought the perception that there's any luck involved in all this, but they don't shy away from the reality that it's peculiar to watch and be a part of.

"(Travis) Ishikawa said this earlier: If there's an unconventional way to win a game, we'll find it," Crawford

said. "But a win is a win. We'll take it."

The Giants embraced convention at times, too, even if those fleeting moments included their own unique twists. Ishikawa had the big early blast, one that goes in the box score as a three-run double off the right-field wall. In real time, it was a crushed shot that was headed for the seats until the wind caught hold of it and dragged it back toward center field. Right fielder Randal Grichuk gave chase but lost the ball and ended up standing a dozen feet away as it bounced off the bottom of an archway and skittered back toward center.

"That's as good as I can hit a ball," Ishikawa said. "Obviously this ballpark and the wind had other ideas."

Every experienced Giants outfielder, from Blanco to Hunter Pence to Juan Perez, said this was the toughest wind day they have seen alongside McCovey Cove. The flags stood stiff for over three hours, gusting balls back toward center field. But in other spots, the wind swirled, or pushed balls toward the scoreboard. The elements would put Pence surprisingly far out of reach when Kolten Wong crushed a triple off the same wall in the fourth, cutting the Cardinals' deficit from four to two.

What had started as a brutal day for John Lackey and an easy one for Tim Hudson turned into another postseason thriller. Lackey gave up just one hit after

BRANDON CRAWFORD CELEBRATES AS HE SCORES THE GAME-WINNING RUN IN THE 10TH INNING OF GAME 3. (NHAT V. MEYER/STAFF)

the first, a single by Hudson that snapped his 0-for-42 skid at the plate. Hudson needed just 39 pitches to get through the first three innings but gave two back to Wong and allowed another run on Jhonny Peralta's single in the sixth.

The bullpen was humming by that point, but manager Bruce Bochy wanted Hudson to get two more outs in the seventh. He got one and then gave up a solo shot to Grichuk, the fifth Cardinals homer of the series to none for the Giants.

Hudson and Lackey were done by the end of the seventh, but a bullpen battle that favored the Cardinals in Game 2 flipped the other way. Jeremy Affeldt, Santiago Casilla, Javier Lopez and Sergio Romo held the Cardinals down for 3⅔ innings, setting the stage for an unlikely rally in the bottom of the 10th.

Choate, the funky southpaw, held lefties to a .093 average this season, but the matchup didn't faze Crawford. He has worked religiously on keeping his front shoulder closed when swinging off lefties, and he hit over 100 points higher against them than righties this season. Choate got two strikes on Crawford, but he fouled off two tough sinkers and worked a crucial eight-pitch walk.

Perez had a rough season, hitting just .170 between trips back to Triple-A Fresno, but he was asked to bunt, not hit, when he followed Crawford. Perez fouled off two straight sinkers as the dugout groaned and he steamed.

"That's one of the jobs I'm here for — I've got to get that bunt down," he said. "I'm a guy off the bench, not playing every day, and Bochy has that confidence in me that I can get the bunt down against anybody."

LEFT-HANDER JEREMY AFFELDT PITCHED 1⅔ SCORELESS INNINGS IN RELIEF OF TIM HUDSON IN GAME 3. (JOSIE LEPE/STAFF)

Having failed miserably, Perez altered his mindset. He told himself that at the very least he had to hit the ball hard somewhere, and four pitches after the second failed bunt attempt, he lined a single into left.

"Now you're playing with house money," Bochy said.

That set up another bunt attempt, and Blanco, like Perez, failed to get his first one down. When the Giants small-balled their way to an NLDS win, Blanco said it was fun to win ugly. How appropriate, then, that it was his second bunt attempt, a perfectly successful one, that led to Choate throwing the ball away, with Crawford racing home as the Giants dugout joyfully spilled onto the field.

They had two hits over the final nine innings and went five straight innings without reaching base before Crawford ignited the winning rally, and yet they walked away winners for the sixth time in eight games this postseason.

"It unfolded just how we planned it," Hudson said. "Just how we drew it up." ■

GIANTS STARTER TIM HUDSON STRUCK OUT FIVE IN 6 ²/₃ INNINGS. (SUSAN TRIPP POLLARD/STAFF)

NATIONAL LEAGUE CHAMPIONSHIP SERIES: GAME 4
OCTOBER 15, 2014 | GIANTS 6, CARDINALS 4

NOT OVER YET

GIANTS NOT COMPLACENT WITH COMMANDING 3-1 LEAD

BY ALEX PAVLOVIC

SAN FRANCISCO—It's the most basic part of the game, the first skill baseball players are taught as toddlers too young to even know what's at stake this time of year. It's the first thing they do every day from spring training until the last gasp of October.

Ballplayers throw.

Except Matt Adams couldn't in the big moments Wednesday, allowing the Giants to race away with another thrilling victory. The first baseman twice failed to get accurate throws off in the sixth inning, and the Giants snatched the lead and never looked back, beating the St. Louis Cardinals 6-4 to take a commanding three-games-to-one advantage in the N. L. Championship Series.

The Giants scored the tying and go-ahead runs on grounders to first, continuing their unconventional ways. Over the last six games, the lineup has scored 22 runs, 12 coming on something other than a base hit. As he sat in his office late Wednesday night, manager Bruce Bochy could do nothing but smile when asked about the seemingly unstoppable ground attack.

"I'd love to have homers mixed in here or there, trust me," he said. "But we're finding that it's not our way right now. It was our way earlier in the year, but we adjusted and guys are doing the little things."

Power has given way to pressure, and opponents continue to crack.

Adams did in the game's biggest moment, making mental and physical mistakes in an inning that will be remembered for his wayward throws but was first defined by a decision that went against the grain. The Giants trailed 4-3 at the time with both starters, Ryan Vogelsong and Shelby Miller, long done for the night. Left-hander Marco Gonzalez ignited the rally with a walk of Juan Perez, a .170 hitter. Brandon Crawford followed with his first hit of the series, and the crowd edged forward as Michael Morse, the man most responsible for that early-season home run barrage, got ready to hit.

But in the dugout, rookie Matt Duffy grabbed a bat adorned with a cartoon Duffman sticker and replaced Morse. With two left-handed hitters — Gregor Blanco and Joe Panik — coming up, the move made most often would be to stick with Morse and hope for a ball in the gap that would tie the game before Gonzales got his left-on-left matchups.

But Bochy opted for bunt over brawn.

"It's the confidence I have in Blanco and Panik — they handle lefties pretty well," Bochy said. "You like your chances."

Duffy has one sacrifice bunt in his short big league

CARDINALS CATCHER A.J. PIERZYNSKI TAGS OUT THE GIANTS' BRANDON BELT AT HOME PLATE IN THE SEVENTH INNING OF GAME 4. (JANE TYSKA/STAFF)

to retreat if the ball was hit to Adams and the first baseman looked home but to break for the plate if he tried for a double play.

It was the kind of throwaway conversation runners have with Flannery hundreds of times a season, just in case, and it would have floated into irrelevance had Panik hit the ball anywhere else. He chopped the ball right at Adams.

"It's kind of funny it happened that way," Crawford said.

Adams tagged first and turned for second, never looking at Crawford, who had gone halfway down the line. "I should have checked," Adams said later. He didn't, and to make matters worse, his throw to second pulled Jhonny Peralta off the bag, meaning there would be no well-turned inning-ending double play, just another run for the Giants.

They added one more on Buster Posey's third RBI of the night, and the bullpen bent but didn't break. The latest strange rally, one Vogelsong said was steeped in "Giants Karma," made a winner of Yusmeiro Petit, who pitched three scoreless innings to stop the bleeding after Vogelsong lasted just three. It edged the Giants one game closer to a third World Series in five seasons.

The Giants were comforted but not comfortable. They needed to take three straight from the Cardinals in the 2012 NLCS to extend their season, and they did. Now, they expect the same fight from the other side.

"We've won three, but that's a number," Bochy said. "It's a number you have to get to before the next one."

With how hard the Giants are pushing, the wait doesn't figure to be a long one. ∎

career and had watched the more experienced Perez fail to get a bunt down the night before. But confidence surged through his body as Bochy sent him up to the plate.

"He doesn't second-guess his decisions, and in turn we don't second-guess ourselves," Duffy said.

The Giants had just 45 sacrifice bunts in the regular season, the lowest total in the National League. Duffy got a high sinker from Gonzales and still put it down, moving both runners over. Bochy believes strongly in pressure leading to postseason mistakes, and with the tying run now on third instead of second, Adams folded.

Cardinals manager Mike Matheny played his infield in to cut off the tying run, and Blanco rewarded him with a two-hopper right at Adams. The lumbering first baseman stumbled and then threw a bouncer to the plate, allowing Perez to slide in safely. When Crawford reached third, he checked in with coach Tim Flannery, who calls Crawford his best base runner — not because of speed but because of instincts. Flannery told Crawford

ABOVE: THE CARDINALS' MATT CARPENTER SLIDES IN SAFELY PAST BRANDON CRAWFORD ON HIS LEADOFF DOUBLE IN THE FIRST INNING. CARPENTER LATER SCORED ON A MATT ADAMS SINGLE AS THE CARDINALS TOOK AN EARLY 1-0 LEAD. (JOSIE LEPE/STAFF) OPPOSITE: GIANTS STARTER RYAN VOGELSONG DELIVERS IN THE FIRST INNING OF GAME 4. VOGELSONG YIELDED SEVEN HITS AND FOUR EARNED RUNS IN THREE INNINGS BEFORE THE GIANTS' BULLPEN SHUT DOWN THE CARDINALS THE REST OF THE WAY. (JOSIE LEPE/STAFF)

CHAMPIONS AGAIN

GIANTS WIN PENNANT ON ISHIKAWA'S HOME RUN

BY ALEX PAVLOVIC

SAN FRANCISCO—Travis Ishikawa spread his arms as the ball soared into the dark sky and screamed even though AT&T Park shook so violently that he couldn't hear himself think, let alone celebrate a homer that put the Giants in the World Series for the third time in five years.

And then, because nothing comes easily for this group of National League champions, Ishikawa hit a roadblock.

As Ishikawa approached third base, his three-run walk-off homer in the ninth having just given the Giants a 6-3 win over the St. Louis Cardinals and a date with the Kansas City Royals, he was confronted by Jake Peavy, who like Ishikawa is one of the season's many unlikely saviors. Peavy's vision is so bad that he can hardly see Buster Posey's signs some nights, and he was still foggy from laughing gas administered during an emergency dental operation needed because he had chipped two teeth trying to open a pack of gum. He didn't realize Ishikawa had homered, so he ran out for a hug, desperate to tell Ishikawa how proud he was.

"Move!" Ishikawa screamed. "I hit it out!"

The ball crept over the fence and into the arcade, permanently washing away the "luck" talk that so dominated this series. Sure, the Giants benefited from a fortuitous bounce or two every night, but with a chance to clinch in Game 5 of the N.L. Championship Series, they got three of the biggest blasts in franchise history, dramatically snapping a streak of 242 plate appearances without a homer.

Joe Panik's first career home run at AT&T Park kept them close. Michael Morse's first in two months tied a game that appeared lost heading to the eighth. Ishikawa's first postseason homer made a hero out of a potential goat after he had botched an earlier play in left field and cost Madison Bumgarner a run. After going six games without a homer, the Giants scored every run Thursday on the long ball.

"I guess we saved the best swings for last," Panik said. "The last couple of games, the bounces were going our way, but tonight we hit our way out of it."

Panik's third-inning homer, just his second in more than 300 big league at-bats, gave the Giants a fresh start. Bumgarner was put to work early, and the Cardinals took a 1-0 lead in the third when Ishikawa, a first baseman his entire life until the past month, misjudged Jon Jay's liner that went over his head and to the wall. Bumgarner didn't seethe, choosing instead to focus on limiting the damage.

"As a pitcher, you take more pride in picking your defense up than anything else," he said.

Ishikawa said he was "feeling as low as I could feel at

TRAVIS ISHIKAWA CELEBRATES AS HE ROUNDS THIRD BASE AFTER HITTING A THREE-RUN WALK-OFF HOME RUN TO WIN GAME 5 AND CLINCH THE NATIONAL LEAGUE PENNANT. (NHAT V. MEYER/STAFF)

that moment," but he returned to the dugout and found that no one would leave him alone. "I can't even call them teammates — they're family," he said later, eyes red not just because of champagne. "Every coach, player and trainer came up and said don't worry about it."

The Giants certainly played like they weren't concerned by the deficit, and soon the misplay would be forgotten. Adam Wainwright had retired Panik three times in Game 1, repeatedly throwing cutters in on his hands. The 23-year-old rookie adjusted Thursday and repeated his game plan in his head after Wainwright missed with a fastball for ball one.

"I was waiting for the cutter," Panik said. "At 1-0, I knew he liked his cutter."

Panik loved it. He crushed the inside pitch out to right for a two-run homer, giving Bumgarner the lead. It would last just a few minutes, as Matt Adams and Tony Cruz hit solo homers off Bumgarner in the fourth. Bolstered by the belief that the lineup would find some way to bounce back against Wainwright, Bumgarner buckled down, retiring the next 13 hitters he faced. The effort, coupled with his Game 1 win, earned Bumgarner the series MVP trophy.

"I don't know that I'm 100 percent deserving," he said. "There are plenty of guys that deserve it, also."

Two more unlikely candidates popped up in the final two innings. After seven strong frames, Wainwright gave way to Pat Neshek, a sidewinding right-hander who was perfect in his first three appearances in this series. As Morse stepped out of the dugout, Posey pulled him back.

"He told me: 'Just touch it, with your strength you can hit a homer,'" Morse recalled, a beer pinned inside his goggles and a disbelieving grin on his face.

Just touch it?

"Look at him — he's 6-foot-6 and built like a house!" Posey said.

Morse floated it over the left field wall and then floated around the bases. The dugout met him with a collective hug, thankful for new life. A dazzling defensive play by Brandon Crawford and yet another big pitch from Jeremy Affeldt got the Giants out of a tense top of the ninth. Pablo Sandoval singled off Michael Wacha in the bottom of the inning, and Brandon Belt walked. Wacha, pitching for the first time this postseason, threw a 96 mph fastball that Ishikawa crushed.

The park erupted, and fireworks went off behind the scoreboard. The dugout emptied and headed for the plate. Hunter Pence said he blacked out. Peavy laughed as he tried to explain why he made a beeline for the man still 90 feet from touching home. Later, they met in a clubhouse corner and shared a long embrace. Ishikawa tried to explain what he had seen. He smiled and shook his head.

"I can't remember anything after the ball going over the fence," he said.

In San Francisco, they'll never let him forget it. ■

THIRD BASEMAN PABLO SANDOVAL STRETCHES TO CATCH A LINE DRIVE OFF THE BAT OF THE CARDINALS' JHONNY PERALTA IN THE FIRST INNING. SANDOVAL THEN THREW OUT JON JAY AT SECOND BASE TO COMPLETE AN INNING-ENDING DOUBLE PLAY. (NHAT V. MEYER/STAFF)

FANS AT AT&T PARK CELEBRATE AFTER HUNTER PENCE SCORED SAN FRANCISCO'S THIRD RUN IN THE FIRST INNING OF THE GIANTS' 9-0 DEFEAT OF THE DODGERS ON SEPT. 12. (D. ROSS CAMERON/STAFF)

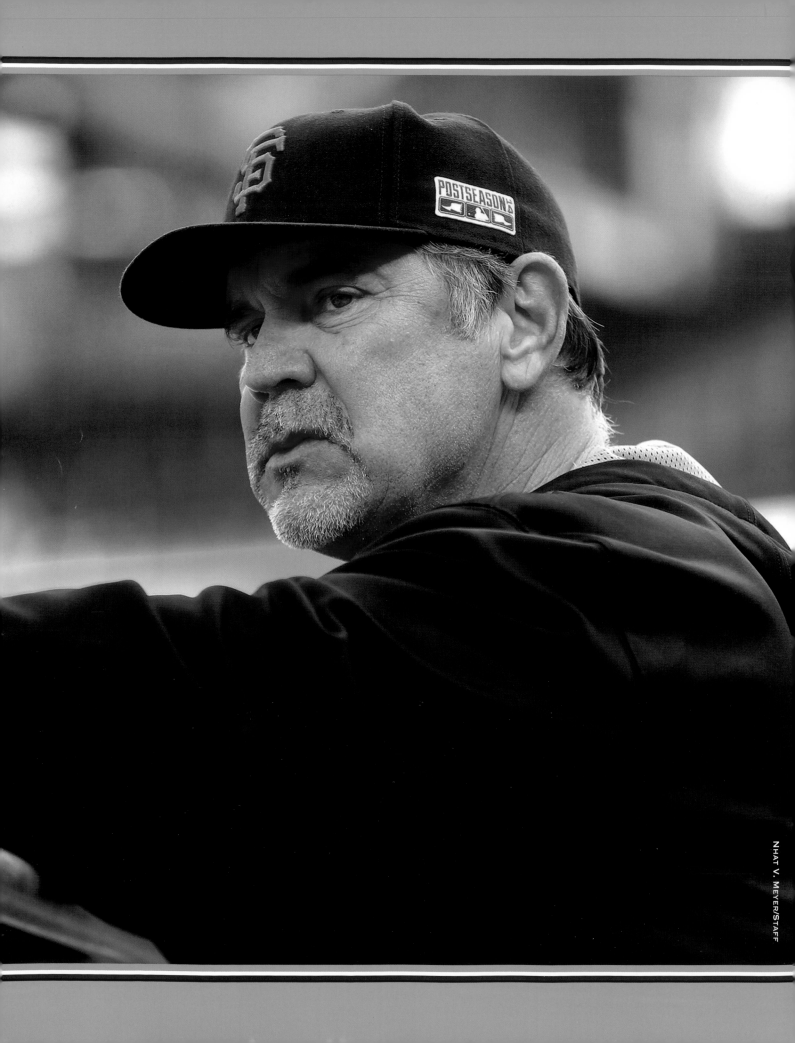